The Ultimate INDOOR GAMES Book

D1055830

The Ultimate INDOOR GAMES Book

The Best Boredom Busters Ever!

Veronika Alice Gunter

Illustrated by
Clay Meyer

LARK BOOKS

A Division of Sterling Publishing Co., Inc.
New York / London

Boca Raton Public Library, Boca Raton, FL

Library of Congress Cataloging-in-Publication Data

Gunter, Veronika Alice.
  The ultimate indoor games book : the best boredom busters ever! / Veronika
Alice Gunter. -- Rev. ed.
      p. cm.
  Includes index.
  ISBN-13: 978-1-60059-198-3 (pb-trade pbk. : alk. paper)
  ISBN-10: 1-60059-198-1 (pb-trade pbk. : alk. paper)
  1. Indoor games--Juvenile literature. I. Title. II. Title: Indoor games
book.
  GV1229.G86 2007
  793--dc22
                              2007005718
10 9 8 7 6 5 4 3 2 1

A different version of this material was previously published in hard cover.

Published by Lark Books, A Division of Sterling Publishing Co., Inc.,
387 Park Avenue South, New York, N.Y. 10016

Text © 2007, Lark Books

Illustrations © 2007, Clay Meyer

Distributed in Canada by Sterling Publishing, c/o Canadian Manda Group,
165 Dufferin Street, Toronto, Ontario, Canada M6K 3H6

Distributed in the United Kingdom by GMC Distribution Services, Castle Place, 166 High Street, Lewes, East Sussex, England BN7 1XU

Distributed in Australia by Capricorn Link (Australia) Pty Ltd., P.O. Box 704, Windsor, NSW 2756 Australia

The written instructions, photographs, designs, patterns, and projects in this volume are intended for the personal use of the reader and may be reproduced for that purpose only. Any other use, especially commercial use, is forbidden under law without written permission of the copyright holder.

Every effort has been made to ensure that all the information in this book is accurate. However, due to differing conditions, tools, and individual skills, the publisher cannot be responsible for any injuries, losses, and other damages that may result from the use of the information in this book.

If you have questions or comments about this book, please contact: Lark Books, 67 Broadway, Asheville, NC 28801 (828) 253-0467

Manufactured in China

All rights reserved

ISBN 13: 978-1-60059-198-3

ISBN 10: 1-60059-198-1

For information about custom editions, special sales, premium and corporate purchases, please contact Sterling Special Sales Department at 800-805-5489 or specialsales@sterlingpub.com.

Art Director: Robin Gregory

Creative Director/Cover Designer: Celia Naranjo

Illustrator: Clay Meyer

Production Assistance: Bradley Norris

Editorial Assistance: Rose McLarney

Contents

Contents

Rainy Day? Go Ahead and Play!

You look out the window, and what do you see? It's raining. Or sleeting. Or maybe you can't see anything when you look out, because it's pitch dark.

You're stuck indoors. But that doesn't mean you've got to put play on hold. You've got **The Ultimate Indoor Games Book** in your hands! Here are 150 of the best boredom busters ever. These are games to play with best friends, new friends, or family.

• Want games that require no equipment or supplies? Turn to the **Just Play** chapter.

• Test yourself or your friends with the collection of **Races & Relays.** Play one-on-one or in teams.

• Use the **Pen & Paper Games** to stump your friends at word play, drawing games, and more.

• Try old-fashioned and unusual games in the **Card Games** chapter. You can even find games to play with incomplete decks of cards.

• Turn to **Ball Games** for one-of-a-kind indoor games that make time fly.

• Tickle your brain and your funny bone with **Brain Games.**

• Ready for simple games that challenge your dexterity? Turn to the chapter called **Marbles, Coins & Stones.**

• Take a chance and choose a game from the **Oddballs** chapter. The games have nothing in common but fun.

Grab a friend, or three, or more. Choose a game (or three, or more). It's time to play!

Getting Started

Where to Play

You can play all these games inside your house—
even Foot Volleyball, Disc Golf, and lots
of fast-moving games. Some games do require
just the right space for a game to work, and
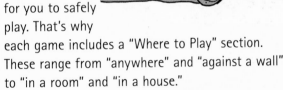
for you to safely
play. That's why
each game includes a "Where to Play" section.
These range from "anywhere" and "against a wall"
to "in a room" and "in a house."

Anytime a game calls for playing "in a room,"
you need to read the instructions, and then
choose a room. So, for Jump Rope Relay on page
99, don't pick a room with a ceiling fan. If you
think you'll make diving catches when you play
500 on page 110, choose a carpeted room. Oh,
and you need to choose a space or room where
you are allowed to play, move furniture, and
remove breakable objects. Always put the room
back the way you found it after you finish playing.

Setting Up Boundaries

These aren't the Olympic games, so the boundaries don't have to be perfect. Just make sure all the players know what the boundaries are so everyone can play fair.

If you need Start and Finish lines, or a Base, sometimes you can use what you have for boundaries. That means you can make the floors, walls, and furniture your boundaries. You can also make adjustments. You could say a rug was Base and move it to just the right location as you set up the play area.

Or, you can mark boundaries using string, rope, or tape. Pick the right material for the game. For instance, you don't want players in a running relay race to trip over a thick rope. Try string or tape instead. (Always get permission before putting tape on the floor; depending on the surface and the type of tape, you could damage the floor.) Dental floss is the best material to use to mark boundaries for marble games; the floss is so thin that the marbles easily roll over it without slowing down.

Equipment

Each game includes a list of "What You Need." You'll find most of this equipment around the house: playing cards, marbles, a bandana. Because you're inside, surrounded by walls, when you play an active game you're more likely to be hit with equipment or bang into friends and doors and such. So you'll find suggestions for equipment that works well for these games indoors. For instance, Foot Volleyball on page 112 uses a balloon for the ball.

Choosing Teams

A game lasts longer and is more fun when you have a balance of ages and sizes on each team, instead of having all the older kids or all the strongest players on one team. Keep this in mind as you pick teams. Here are two random methods for choosing teams:

• Players line up and take turns saying "one" and "two." The Ones are a team. The Twos are the other team. (For three teams, count up to three. And so on.)

• Choose a player to be the Leader who assigns players to an Even or Odd team by having a "shootout" with each player. How a shootout works: the Leader and one player count aloud to three. On "three" the Leader and the player extend either one or two fingers each (index finger or index finger plus middle finger). The total number of fingers pointed determines which team that player joins. (Two is Even; three is Odd; four is Even.) After all the shootouts, the Leader joins whichever team has fewer members. If the teams are equal, the Leader joins the Odds.

Rules

Read the instructions to figure out the rules of a game before you start playing it. Go over the instructions with all the players before you start playing the game. If anything is unclear, agree on how you will handle it.

One of the best things about playing games is that you can make up your own rules. Just add or change rules before the game starts. Or, if the game is too easy or too hard, call a time out and figure out what kind of new rules would make the game more fun. Then start over.

Choosing Referees

Some of the games in this book need a Referee. If you have an extra player waiting a turn to play, have her or him referee. Or ask whether someone wants to take a break from playing and volunteer. You can also try to find an adult to referee. If no one wants to referee, choose someone using the Choosing IT method. Then decide how you'll rotate who's Referee so that everybody gets to play for a while.

Choosing IT

Being IT is fun. And it's easier to catch people when you are IT for an indoor game than for an outdoor game: the players don't have as much room to run from you! Some of these games require one player to be IT. There are lots of ways to pick IT. Here are two:

• Grab a broom or yardstick. Gather around the broom. One person should hold the broom up with a hand at the bottom, nearest the bristles. Quickly, all of the other players place their hands on the broom handle, one hand at a time, until there's no more room. The person with a hand at the top wins.

• Tear up pieces of paper and mark one with an X. Put the papers into a hat so no one can see which piece players draw. The person who gets the X is IT. (This method is perfect for games that require keeping IT's identify secret, such as Winks on page 204.)

Being a Good Sport

The point of playing is to have fun. When every player plays fair, plays hard, and has a good time, everyone is happy. Who wins and who loses doesn't matter. If you lose a game, or two, or 10, so what? If you're having fun, you'll play again. For most of these games, determining who won is just a way to decide who goes first the next time you play. That doesn't mean you shouldn't be pleased if you win a game through skill, effort, or luck. It's a thrill to win. Just don't rub it in. (Have you noticed that a Bad Sport is rarely invited to play again?)

If one player's skills are much better than the rest of the players, consider making a rule to make it more challenging for that player. So, if you're playing Bocce on page 111 and a much older kid has scored all the points, make a rule that players over a certain age have to play using just one hand—their nondominant hand!

How to End the Game

You can play until a goal is reached, such as tagging everyone, or earning 15 points. Either way, figure out what the goal is before you start playing, and how to reach it. (What counts as a point? How many points? What counts as a tag?)

For most of these games, you could play a World Series. Just play an odd-numbered series of games (five, seven, etc.) and see who wins most often. If you don't want to play for a score, play for a specific amount of time, such as "until dinnertime."

Grab your friends, pick a game, play fair, play hard, and have fun!

JUST PLAY

Ready to laugh, hide, wrestle, and more?

Alligator

Number of Players: 3 or more
What You Need: nothing
Where to Play: in a hallway
The Point: avoid the jaws of the Alligator

What You Do

1. One player is the Alligator. Her arms and hands are powerful jaws full of sharp teeth. The Alligator uses her teeth to capture Poachers. All the other players are Poachers.

2. The Alligator kneels in the middle of the hallway. Her knees can't move from that spot during play. The Poachers must pass the Alligator, one at a time or all at once.

3. A Poacher can try to wiggle free, but has to give up if the Alligator locks her jaws around him by clasping her hands. Captured Poachers sit behind the Alligator.

4. The other Poachers continue passing back and forth. The last Poacher captured is the new Alligator. Play again.

Other Ways to Play

Blindfolded: Use a bandana to blindfold the Alligator.

Angels

Number of Players: 6 or more
What You Need: nothing
Where to Play: in a room
The Point: feel the presence of Angels

What You Do

1 Two or three players are Angels. The Angels move to one side of the room.

2 All the others are Mortals. They spread out around the room, find a place to stand, and close their eyes.

3 The Angels count aloud from one to 10. At "10," the Angels quietly move around the room.

4 Each Angel stands as close as possible to a Mortal for 10 seconds. If the Mortal doesn't notice the Angel, the Angel taps the Mortal on the shoulder and the Mortal sits down and is Out. (That Mortal can open both eyes and watch the rest of the players continue the game.)

5 If a Mortal feels an Angel's presence, the Mortal says, "Is there an Angel with me?" If the Mortal is correct, the Angel says so and that Mortal becomes an Angel. If the Mortal is wrong, the Mortal sits down and is Out.

6 Play until everyone is either an Angel or Out.

Arm Wrestling

Number of Players: 2
What You Need: a table and 2 chairs
Where to Play: on a tabletop
The Point: pin your opponent

What You Do

1 Players sit up straight and face their opponent across the table (or across the corner of the table if the table is too large).

2 Players place their right elbows on the tabletop, and clasp one another's right hand as shown in the illustration.

3 Players count down from three together and then use all their arm strength to force the back of the opponent's right hand onto the tabletop. The right elbows and left hands should not move.

4 A player wins by pinning the opponent's hand to the table. Play an odd number of times to see who wins most often.

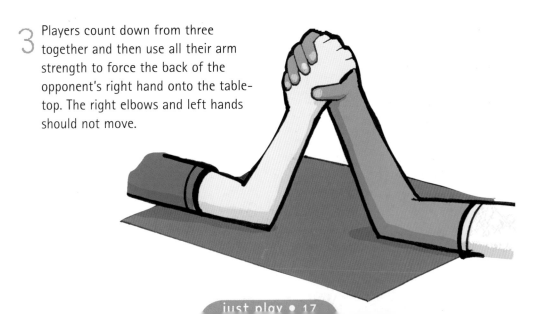

Belly Laugh

Number of Players: 5 or more
What You Need: nothing
Where to Play: in a carpeted room
The Point: keep up with the laughs

What You Do

1 One player lies down on the floor, with her back on the floor. A second player lies down on the floor, resting her head on the belly of the first player.

2 Players continue lying down in this fashion until everyone is on the floor.

3 The first player laughs, "Ha!" The second player must laugh, "Ha, Ha!" The laugh continues down the line, with each player adding a "Ha."

4 Play until somebody laughs at the wrong time, or the wrong way. Then let another player begin passing the laughter. Have fun!

Bumper Cars

What You Do

1 Players squat and tuck their arms behind their thighs so that each hand crosses under and reaches the opposite side. (Players can tuck their arms behind their knees if they prefer.)

2 When everyone's ready, play begins. Each player waddles around and tries to bump the others so they come untucked or fall to the carpet. Players who lose their grip or fall are out of the game. No elbowing or head butting allowed.

3 The last player still in the game wins.

Number of Players: 2 or more
What You Need: nothing
Where to Play: in a carpeted room
The Point: knock your opponent over

Friend or Foe?

Number of Players: 6 or more
What You Need: nothing
Where to Play: in a room
The Point: rejoin your Friends

What You Do

1. One player is IT. The other players stand in a circle and join hands. These joined players are Friends.

2. To begin the game, IT runs around the circle and picks a pair of hands to tap. These two players are now Foes.

3. Each Foe runs in the opposite direction of the opponent, all the way around the circle, racing to rejoin the circle first. Meanwhile, IT becomes a Friend and joins the circle in one of the two open spots.

4. The first Foe to reach the single open spot in the circle is safe and becomes a Friend again. The slower Foe is the new IT.

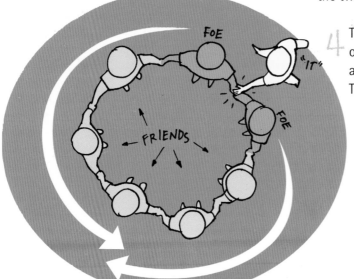

Kick-Off

Number of Players: 2 or more
What You Need: nothing
Where to Play: in a room
The Point: "kick" a winning move

What You Do

1 Two players compete at a time. The players stand and face one another, leaving a few feet of space between them. One player is called "Odd" and the other is called "Even."

2 The players count aloud together from one to three and jump up on each count. After saying, "three," each player "kicks" one of two moves: stick out the right foot or stick out the left foot.

3 If the players' "kicked" feet are lined up toe-to-toe with each other, they're "even." Even wins the round. (This happens when one player kicks out a right foot and the other player kicks out a left foot.) If the players' feet are at a diagonal, they're "odd." Odd wins the round. (This happens when both players kick out their right feet, or both kick out their left feet.)

4 The winner does the count for the next game.

Flamingos

Number of Players: 2
What You Need: nothing
Where to Play: in a carpeted room
The Point: unbalance the other bird

What You Do

1. Players stand facing one another. Each player extends the right arm and hand, and grasps the opponent's extended right hand.

2. It will look as if the players are shaking hands. Then each player bends the left leg, lifts the ankle toward the back, and grasps the left ankle with the left hand. (Bending the right leg can help the player maintain balance more easily.) The stance of both players should now resemble flamingos.

3. On the count of three, players tug and twist their joined hands to unbalance the opponent. The player who makes the other let go of an ankle or break the handhold wins.

Freaky Fingers

What You Do

Number of Players: 4 or more
What You Need: bandana
Where to Play: in a room
The Point: keep quiet

1 One player is IT. IT leaves the room and begins counting to 22. All the other players hide in the room. (To make the game spooky, play at night with the lights off.)

2 IT yells, "22, 22, Freaky Fingers are coming to find you." IT then closes both eyes, puts on the bandana as a blindfold, and reenters the room to search for players. IT should reach out and poke around dramatically with IT's Freaky Fingers. Players can't move!

3 Players should be quiet—IT can't see, but IT can hear. A player touched by IT is Out. The last player found and touched by IT becomes the new IT.

Lazybones

What You Do

1. One player is the Motivational Speaker. (That's a person who encourages others to do something besides being a Lazybones.) All the other players are Lazybones.

2. The Lazybones lie down, stretch out, or curl up in the room. They can keep their eyes open, but they cannot move. (They're too lazy to move!)

3. To win, the Motivational Speaker needs to rouse all the Lazybones, making the Lazybones move just by talking to them. Smiling is moving, and so is changing position.

4. The last Lazybones to move is the next Motivational Speaker.

Number of Players: 3 or more
What You Need: nothing
Where to Play: in a room
The Point: rouse the Lazybones

Can't Move Me

What You Do

1 Players stand and face one another. Each player extends the right foot so that it touches the outside right edge of the other player's right foot.

2 Players clasp each other's right hand, as if shaking hands, and put their left arms behind their backs. Players bend both legs slightly, for balance, and choose a stance.

3 When play begins, players push, pull, and shake the opponent's right hand in an attempt to make the opponent move. The first player to make the other take a step or move the left arm from behind the back wins.

Number of Players: 2
What You Need: nothing
Where to Play: in a carpeted room
The Point: topple your opponent

Other Ways to Play

Switch: Have each player extend the left foot, clasp the opponent's left hand, and put the right hand behind the back.

Hot Lava

What You Do

1. The floor in every room of the house is hot lava. (That includes wood, tile, and carpeting.) Before beginning, players must agree whether or not rugs are part of the lava. One player is the Guide who will lead the others though the house.

2. Players must climb on furniture and step on anything that is not lava. If the Guide gets stuck and can't find a route, or steps in the lava, he loses his job. Then any other player can suggest an idea for continuing. If it works, that player becomes the new Guide.

Number of Players: 2 or more
What You Need: nothing
Where to Play: in a house
The Point: step over the molten rock

3. Any player who touches the lava three times gets a deadly burn and is out of the game. Play until only one player remains. That player is the Guide for the next game.

In or Out?

What You Do

1 Players agree on a line in the room, or mark one with a string. One player is the Leader. The other players all line up on the same side of the agreed-upon line.

2 The Leader tells the players which side of the line is "In" and which is "Out." To begin the game, the Leader counts from one to three out loud, then begins calling out "In" or "Out." The players must jump where they are told.

Number of Players: 4 or more
What You Need: string (optional)
Where to Play: anywhere
The Point: listen closely

(Sometimes this means a player just jumps up and lands in place, instead of jumping over the line.) Anyone who messes up is out of the game.

3 The last player in the game becomes the new Leader.

Chair

What You Do

1 Players stand in a circle, shoulder to shoulder and facing the circle's center.

2 Players all turn to the right and count aloud from one to three. After "three," all players sit down on the knees of the person behind them. Everyone sits at the same time, slowly.

3 To win, everyone must be seated and balanced. Try as many times as it takes to get it right!

Number of Players: 8 or more
What You Need: nothing
Where to Play: in a carpeted room
The Point: sit down in a circle

Other Ways to Play

Forward: After mastering how to sit as a circle, players stay in a seated position and take a step forward.

Backward: After mastering how to sit and take a step forward as a group, the players all take a step backward.

Knots......

Number of Players: 5 or more
What You Need: nothing
Where to Play: anywhere
The Point: untangle yourselves

What You Do

1 All of the players stand in a circle, facing each other. Everybody reaches both hands into the center.

2 Each player grabs hands with the other players, following these rules: no one can hold both hands of another player, and a no one can hold hands with a player to her immediate right or left in the circle. When all the hands are grasped, the whole group will be in a big knot.

3 Start to untangle the knot without letting go of any hands. Players will have to step over and under other players' arms, and twist around.

4 The game is over when everyone is standing in a circle again, still holding hands. Everyone wins!

Part to Part

What You Do

1 One player is the Caller. The other players pair up in teams. (Any extra player can join in during step 3.)

2 The Caller calls out two arm or leg parts at a time and each team must quickly put those parts together. For instance, "ankle to wrist," and then "elbow to knee," then "fingers to foot."

3 At any time, the Caller can say, "person to person." That means all players have to find a new partner as quickly as possible, including the Caller. Whichever player does not get a partner becomes the new Caller.

Number of Players: an odd number of 5 or more

What You Need: nothing

Where to Play: in a room

The Point: make silly connections

4 Play until everyone has had a turn as the Caller.

Pinkie Pairs ......

What You Do

1 Players pair up, stand back-to-back with their hands to their sides, and then link their pinkies.

2 Each pair must lower to the floor, pressing against the back of the partner. Pairs go all the way to the floor, until both players are sitting, and then get back up. Backsides must touch the whole time. Pinkies can't come unlinked.

3 The pairs of players who succeed are the winners. (More than one team can win.)

Number of Players: 2 or more
What You Need: nothing
Where to Play: in a room
The Point: slide down, then up

Leg Wrestling

What You Do

1 Players lie on the floor, heads aligned with feet. (See illustration.) Legs and arms are outstretched down alongside their bodies, nearly touching the opponent. Players' backs must remain flat against the floor throughout the game.

2 Players link arms at the elbow, using the nearest arm. The other arm remains on the floor.

3 Players extend the leg nearest the opponent straight up toward the ceiling, and then link this leg behind the knee of the opponent's extended leg.

4 On the count of three, the game begins and players wrestle, using only their linked legs and arms.

Number of Players: 2 of similar size
What You Need: nothing
Where to Play: on a carpeted floor
The Point: outmuscle the competition

5 A player wins by forcing the opponent's back off the floor. Players should play fair and announce when their backs raise. Assign a Referee if necessary.

Rock Paper Scissors

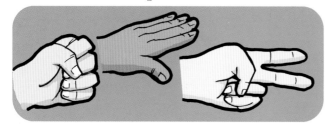

What You Do

1. Players can "throw" one of three gestures in this game. The possible throws are Rock, formed by making a fist; Paper, formed by flattening the hand, palm down; or Scissors, formed by opening the middle and index fingers to resemble a pair of scissors.

2. Rock always breaks Scissors to win, Paper always covers Rock to win, and Scissors always cuts Paper to win. Players can also tie by throwing the same gesture.

Number of Players: 2 or more
What You Need: nothing
Where to Play: anywhere
The Point: make a winning gesture

3. Players face one another and count out loud together from one to three, each player hitting one fist into the palm of his other hand on each count.

4. After the third hit, each player "throws" a gesture, using the top fist. The winner does the count for the next game. If the players tie, those players throw again until one wins.

Sardines

What You Do

Number of Players: 4 or more
What You Need: good places to hide
Where to Play: in a house
The Point: everyone squeezes in

1 Players agree on a Base and choose the one player who will go hide. All the other players stand at Base, cover their eyes, and count together to 30.

2 When the counting is finished, everyone separates and looks for the hiding spot. Each player who finds the hiding spot (and the hiding player) squeezes in to hide, too.

3 The last one to find the hiding spot is chased back to Base by the rest of the players. If that player is caught, she becomes the next player to hide. Otherwise, the second-to-last player who found the hiding spot hides next.

Shipshape

Number of Players: 3 or more
What You Need: nothing
Where to Play: in a room
The Point: obey or Walk the Plank

What You Do

1. The room is a Ship. One player is the Captain. The other players are the Pirates who work for the Captain.

2. The game begins when the Captain says, "All Pirates on deck." That means all players need to stand up for duty. The Captain will give the following commands in any order:

   Hit the deck: Lay down on the floor

   Stern: Run to the back

   Row your boat: The Captain points to three players and they sing, "Row, Row, Row Your Boat"

   Clear the deck: Pirates can't touch the floor with their feet

   Starboard: Run to the right side

   Port: Run to the left side

   Bow: Run to the front

   Attention: Stand, salute, and say, "Aye, aye, Captain"

3. If the Captain sees a Pirate not following orders, the Captain commands the Pirate to Walk the Plank, and the Pirate is automatically Out. The last remaining Pirate becomes the new Captain.

Stop and Go

What You Do

1 Pick the first player to be IT and mark the Start Line. IT stands far away from all the other players, who line up just behind the Start Line.

2 IT calls out, "green light," and turns IT's back to the players. The players begin walking quickly toward IT. No running allowed. IT calls out "red light," spins and faces the players—who freeze. Anyone IT catches moving goes back to Start. Then IT calls out "green light" again, and so on.

Number of Players: 3 or more
What You Need: string (optional)
Where to Play: in a wide hallway or room
The Point: reach IT

3 The first player to touch IT wins and becomes the new IT.

Super Duck

Number of Players: 4 or more
What You Need: nothing
Where to Play: in a house
The Point: be a superhero, or foil one!

What You Do

1. Players agree on a playing area, such as three connected rooms in the house. Players pick someone to be IT, and IT picks a space to be the Prison, such as on an area rug in the kitchen.

2. All the players stand in the Prison, or with at least one foot in. While IT closes both eyes and counts aloud to 10, the other players run from the Prison and hide. After reaching "10," IT hunts for the players.

3. When IT sees or touches a player, that player must go to the Prison. At any time any Prisoner can call out, "This is a job for Super Duck." Any other player can reply with a loud "quack quack." This frees the Prisoner. But look out, because now IT has heard a clue to at least one player's whereabouts!

4. IT wins by capturing all the players in the Prison. (It's hard to win!)

Crawling Tag

Number of Players: 3 or more
What You Need: nothing
Where to Play: in a large room
The Point: keep moving

What You Do

1 Pick a person to be IT. IT must crawl on all fours, and begins play in the middle of the room.

2 The other players line up against one end of the room. That wall is Start. The opposite wall is Base. IT yells "go" and play begins. Players must alternate touching Base and Start—by getting past IT. (A player who fails to alternate touching Base and Start is automatically the new IT!)

3 IT tags players, and wherever IT touches a player, the player has to stick her hand there. For instance, IT could tag her ankle. She can move, but she has to keep the hand on her ankle until another player touches the same spot and "frees" the "stuck" hand. IT can only tag each player once on each of the player's trips between Start and Base.

4 IT can tag any player who has a "free" hand—unless the player is touching Start or Base. Being tagged three times makes a player the next IT!

Thumbs Up

What You Do

1 The players close their eyes and count out loud together from one to three. On "three," the players each stick both of their fists out and do one of the following: stick up one thumb, two thumbs, or no thumbs.

2 With eyes still closed, each player quickly calls out a number that is a guess of how many thumbs will be up. If someone cheats and peeks, restart the game and do Step 2 first, followed by Step 1.

Number of Players: 4 or more
What You Need: nothing
Where to Play: anywhere
The Point: guess well

3 The players all open their eyes and count the thumbs. The player who guessed correctly wins. (Sometimes no one wins.) Play an odd number of times to see who wins most often.

Thumb Wrestling

What You Do

1. Each player makes a fist with the right hand and rests the right forearm on the table. The hand is pinky-side down and players should face one another.

2. Players open those fists just enough to grip the opponent's fingers. Each player rests a thumb near the knuckle of his own index finger.

3. The players count down aloud together from three. On "one," the Wrestling begins. The right hands must remain clasped, and the right forearms must remain on the table.

Number of Players: 2
What You Need: nothing
Where to Play: on a table
The Point: pin the opponent's thumb

4. The first player to pin the other's thumb and hold it for a count of three wins. If necessary, assign a Referee to do the counting.

Other Ways to Play

Declaration: Recite "One, two, three, four, I declare a thumb war!" while giving alternating thumb taps to each right index-finger knuckle. Then start Wrestling.

Sock Wrestling

What You Do

1 Players pair up and take off their shoes. Pairs can sit or stand, but it's easiest to start the game sitting on your heels.

2 Players count aloud together from one to three. On "three," they begin trying to take off the opponent's socks. Players shouldn't play too rough. Have fun!

3 The first player to get both socks off the opponent's feet wins.

Number of Players: 2 or more
What You Need: socks on your feet
Where to Play: in a carpeted room
The Point: remove your opponent's socks

Wily Knights

Number of Players: 2 or more
What You Need: nothing
Where to Play: in a room
The Point: score points with finger swords

What You Do

1 Players pair up and stand facing one another. (An extra player can play against the winner of the first game.)

2 Players put one hand behind their backs, laying the back of the hand flat against the back, with the palm open. This is the Knight's Shield. It must stay behind the back in the position described. The index finger of the other hand is the Knight's Sword.

3 Players count together to three. On three, each Knight tries to "strike" (touch) the opponent's Shield with her Sword. Touching any part of the opponent's palm counts as a strike and earns a point. Players should move around to play but running and leaving the room aren't allowed.

4 The first Knight to earn seven points wins. Play an odd number of times and see who wins most often.

BRAIN GAMES

Think fast, think hard, think fun!

A What?

What You Do

1. The players sit in a circle. One player begins the game by passing an object to the left, announcing that it's something completely different. For instance, pass a football while saying, "This is a hot extra-cheese pizza."

2. The second player must ask, "A what?" The first player repeats, "A hot extra-cheese pizza." The second player then takes the object and passes it to the next player, using the same dialogue. ("This is a hot extra-cheese pizza." "A what?" "A hot extra-cheese pizza.")

3. The first object keeps going around the circle, but now the first player adds a second object to the game, passing it in either direction (right or left). Again, the object is called something it's not. (Make sure you call it something silly and complicated.) Now two objects are being passed.

4. Keep adding objects and passing them until everyone is laughing—or until players can pass four objects twice around the circle without a single mistake.

Number of Players: 5 or more

What You Need: football, water bottle, book, or other objects

Where to Play: in a room

The Point: keep track of which what is what

Animal Vegetable Mineral

What You Do

1 One player is the Answerer, and the others are all Guessers. The Answerer picks the subject of the game, which must fall under one of these categories: Animal, Vegetable, or Mineral.

Animal: an animal (including a specific person) or a thing made from an animal (Swiss cheese, a type of leather shoes)

Vegetable: a vegetable or things made from vegetables (paper, clothes, French fries)

Mineral: everything else (the Statue of Liberty, roads, air)

Number of Players: 3 or more
What You Need: nothing
Where to Play: anywhere
The Point: figure out the answer

2 The Guessers try to figure out the subject by taking turns asking a total of 20 questions. The Answerer responds only with a "yes" or "no."

3 After all 20 questions are asked, each Guesser takes a turn guessing what the subject is. The winner is the first Guesser to get it right.

Antidisestablishmentarianism

What You Do

1 One player is IT. Players take turns asking IT questions. IT's only answer to every question is "Antidisestablishmentarianism."

2 That's "an-ti-dis-es-tab-lish-men-tar-ian-ism." The "tar" is pronounced like "tear" as in "to rip." (Why did the chicken cross the road? "Antidisestablishmentarianism.")

3 The first player to make IT mess up saying the word or laugh at a question becomes the new IT.

Number of Players: 3 or more
What You Need: nothing
Where to Play: anywhere
The Point: make IT laugh or mess up

Other Ways to Play

Soysage: Use "soysage" or another funny word as the answer to all the questions.

Three-Letter Words

What You Do

1 One player says a three-letter word, and then creates a sentence or string of words using the letters of the word. For instance, "Dog: Did Opal go?"

2 Play passes to the left, with each player using that same word and making up a new sentence or string of words. Players who mess up are Out.

3 The last person to take a turn without messing up wins and gets to pick the next three-letter word.

Number of players: 2 or more
What You Need: nothing
Where to Play: anywhere
The Point: blurt out silly strings of words

Other Ways to Play

Lightning round: Choose a timekeeper to limit each player to only 10 seconds or less to respond.
Add letters: Use words with four letters.
Go backward: Create a backward sentence or phrase. For instance, "Dog: Go out, Doug."

Campfire

What You Do

1. Players sit in a circle. One player is the Leader. The other players are the Campers. The Leader begins a story of a hike and the Campers use their hands to make the sound of what the Leader describes. These are the sounds and how to create them:

   Walking: Campers slap their legs in a slow, steady rhythm.

   Crossing a bridge: Campers slap their hands on the floor.

   Climbing a mountain: Campers slap their hands together over their heads.

   Swimming across a river: Campers make swimming motions with their hands.

2. At any time, the Leader can alter the story to say the Campers ran into a bear. The Campers must race back to camp by traveling the same ways and making the right sounds and movements in the correct reverse order. The Leader is the judge of who gets the order correct.

3. The first Camper to get back to camp is the new Leader.

Number of Players: 3 or more
What You Need: nothing
Where to Play: anywhere
The Point: race to camp with your hands

Bean Soup

Number of Players: 7 or more
What You Need: nothing
Where to Play: in a room
The Point: mix the soup without getting left out

What You Do

1 One player is IT and stands in the center of the room. The other players stand in a line near IT.

2 IT assigns a unique vegetable name to each player, such as green beans, okra, and so on. Players must remember their names.

3 To begin the game, IT announces for two players to switch places in line. For instance "Green Beans and Okra, switch."

4 While the players called on move as quickly as possible to switch places, IT tries to take one of their spots.

5 Whoever doesn't get a spot becomes IT and the old IT takes that player's name. (Artichoke?) Play until everyone has been IT.

Beep-Beep, Buzz-Buzz

What You Do

1. The players sit in a circle. There are two sounds and two ways to pass them:

   Beep-beep: put a hand on the head with a finger pointing straight ahead.

   Buzz-buzz: put a hand under the chin and point a finger right or left.

2. One player starts the game by passing a sound. The player pointed at must catch it by doing the same action, and then quickly pass a sound with the other hand. Players use only one hand at a time.

Number of Players: 2 or more
What You Need: nothing
Where to Play: in a room
The Point: pass the sound

3. If a player messes up, she starts again. Everyone wins when the whole group completes making passes to each player.

Lies & Truths

What You Do

1 Players take turns telling two Truths and one Lie. The person taking a turn is the Confessor. The Confessor should decide what to say and then tell the Truths and Lie in any order.

2 The game is really fun when you pick Truths that your friends don't know, and a Lie that sounds ordinary. For instance, "I swam naked in the city pool," "I like butter on mashed potatoes," and "I am named after my aunt." The answers are True (but I was only two years old!), False (butter is gross!), True (she was my great-aunt, but that's still an aunt).

Number of Players: 3 or more
What You Need: nothing
Where to Play: anywhere
The Point: reveal the lies

3 The other players have to agree on which of the three is the Lie. If the players are correct, one of them takes a turn as Confessor. If they are wrong, the Confessor gets another turn.

Poodle

What You Do

1. One player is the Poodler. The Poodler thinks of an action, such as "bicycling" or "thinking," and keeps it a secret. This action is now known as "poodling."

2. When the Poodler is ready, the other players take turns asking the Poodler "yes" and "no" questions to figure out the action. Players might ask, "Can anyone poodle?", "Does poodling hurt?", or "Do you poodle in public?"

Number of Players: 3 or more
What You Need: nothing
Where to Play: anywhere
The Point: figure out what it means to "poodle"

3. Each player can make a guess after asking a question. The first player to figure out what it means to "poodle" wins and is the new Poodler.

Hurrah!

What You Do

1. Pick a player to be IT. IT goes away from all the other players while they huddle and agree on a pose, such as sitting with legs crossed, lying down with one leg in the air, etc.

2. When the other players are ready, IT comes back and slowly begins moving IT's arms, legs, and body into different positions. If IT is getting close to the agreed-on position, all the other players clap and cheer. If IT is not, the players boo.

Number of Players: 3 or more
What You Need: nothing
Where to Play: anywhere
The Point: decipher the cheers and boos

3. When IT finally gets the pose right, the players cheer wildly and shout "Hurrah!"

So You Think You Know Your ABCs?

What You Do

1 Players begin by saying, "So you think you know your ABCs?" and then recite the alphabet—backward. All players speak at the same time.

2 Anyone who messes up must start again, repeating, "So you think you know your ABCs?"

3 A player wins by getting to the letter A without a mistake.

Number of Players: 2 or more
What You Need: nothing
Where to Play: anywhere
The Point: reverse the alphabet

Other Ways to Play

Take turns: Players can take turns if they have trouble reciting their ABCs all at the same time. Just remember the last letter each player recited correctly. Let the player who gets closest to the letter A be the winner.

Story......

What You Do

1. Players stand or sit in a circle. One player is the Storyteller. All the other players are Characters.

2. The game begins when the Storyteller starts telling a story, making it up on the spot. For every Character in the story, the Storyteller points to a player. That player becomes that Character.

3. Every time a Character is mentioned, the player representing that Character has to act out what is happening while walking once around the circle. Walking around the circle gives the

Character more room to pantomime the action. The Storyteller can also say "all," and all the Characters have to act out and walk around the circle.

4. When the story is over, pick a new Storyteller.

> **Number of Players:** 5 or more
> **What You Need:** nothing
> **Where to Play:** in a room
> **The Point:** listen for your role and play your part

Count Down

What You Do

1 Players count backward and out loud from 100 (100, 99, 98, 97, etc.). All players count at the same time. That's what makes the game hard.

2 Anyone who messes up must start over at 100 again. It doesn't matter how many times players mess up, they must start over each time.

3 A player wins by counting down to zero without a mistake.

Number of Players: 2 or more
What You Need: nothing
Where to Play: anywhere
The Point: think in reverse

Other Ways to Play

Take turns: Players can take turns if they have trouble counting all at the same time. Just remember the last number each player counted correctly. Let the player who gets closest to zero be the winner.

By Twos: Count backward by twos. (100, 98, 96, 94, etc.)

By Fives: Count backward by fives. (100, 95, 90, 85, etc.)

I Spy

Number of Players: 2 or more
What You Need: nothing
Where to Play: anywhere
The Point: listen and look

What You Do

1. One player is the Seer. The Seer looks around and chooses an inanimate object (not a person or animal). The object must be in plain sight in the agreed-upon play area. The Seer should avoid drawing anyone's attention to the object.

2. When the Seer is ready, he gives a hint about the object. For instance, if the Seer has chosen a green pillow, he could say, "I spy something green."

3. The other players take one turn each guessing what object the Seer is talking about. If no one guesses correctly, the Seer gives another simple clue. For instance, "I spy something soft."

4. Each time the Seer gives a hint, each player gets one chance to guess what the object is. The first player to guess correctly wins.

Susan B. Anthony

Number of Players: 5 or more
What You Need: nothing
Where to Play: in a room
The Point: keep track of who's talking next

What You Do

1 Players sit in a circle for this word passing game. One player starts the game by looking at another player and saying, "Susan."

2 It's now that player's turn either to look at a different player and say, "B.," or to send the turn right back to the other player by looking away and saying, "Anthony."

3 If a turn is immediately sent back, that receiving player has two options: say "Susan" while looking at a new/different player, or say, "B.," while looking anywhere and sending the turn back to the player who said "Anthony."

4 Let everyone have a turn and play until everyone is hopelessly confused.

No Way

What You Do

1 Pick a player to be the Talker and stand him at one end of the room. Everyone else is a Walker and lines up side by side at the opposite end of the room.

2 Each Walker wants to get to the Talker first, and the Talker wants to keep all the Walkers away. When play begins, each Walker takes a turn asking, "Talker, may I take a step?"

3 The Talker can say "Yes" or "No," but can't say "No" the same way twice. ("Nope." " I don't think so." "Negative.") If the talker can't find a new way to say "No" within 5 seconds, the Talker has to say, "Yes." Then that Walker may take a step of any size.

4 A Talker wins by keeping the Walkers away. A Walker wins by making the Talker say "No" the same way twice, or by getting close enough to touch the Talker.

Other Ways to Play

Nein: Say no in other languages. Nein (German), Geen (Dutch), Non (French), Ingen (Norwegian).

Number of Players: 3 or more
What You Need: nothing
Where to Play: in a room or wide hallway
The Point: stretch your vocabulary

Rainstorm

What You Do

1 Players stand in a circle. One player is the Rainmaker. The Rainmaker begins the game by making a sound that you hear during a rainstorm: falling rain, gusts of wind, thunder, etc. The Rainmaker should make the sounds in his throat, with his fingers or hands, or by stomping his feet, etc.

2 The sound passes around the circle to the left, and each player makes the sound the same way until everyone in the circle is making the same sound. Then the Rainmaker creates a new sound, and it moves around the circle.

Number of Players: 4 or more
What You Need: nothing
Where to Play: in a room
The Point: re-create a storm inside

3 After at least one round of play, any player may yell "Kaboom!" to make lightning strike. When someone yells, "Kaboom," everyone falls down. The fastest player to the floor is the new Rainmaker.

Zombie

Number of Players: 3 or more
What You Need: nothing
Where to Play: in a room
The Point: keep still or be turned into a Zombie

What You Do

1. One player is a Zombie. Every other player is a Corpse. The Zombie is hunting for Corpses that aren't really dead.

2. Before the game begins, the Corpses spread out around the room and lie down. Corpses avoid capture by pretending to be dead and not moving.

3. The Zombie can't touch the Corpses, but the Zombie can talk to Corpses to make them move. Laughing, smiling, opening your eyes, and cringing all count as moves.

4. If the Zombie sees a Corpse move, the Zombie captures the Corpse and it becomes a Zombie. The new Zombie helps the first Zombie search for more moving Corpses.

RACES & RELAYS

Compete with your brain, hands, or feet.

Centipede

Number of Players: 6 or more

What You Need: 1 balloon per team, string (optional)

Where to Play: in a room or hallway

The Point: cross the finish

What You Do

1. Players agree on a Finish Line across the middle of the room, or mark one with string. Players then divide into teams of at least three players each.

2. The teams stand side by side on one end of the room in two single-file lines, so they resemble two Centipedes facing the Finish Line. The player at the front of each Centipede line holds a balloon.

3. To begin the race, each first player lifts the balloon overhead and hands it back to the second player. Each second player passes the balloon between his legs to the third player. Players on both teams alternate over-head and between-the-legs passes until the balloon reaches the last player in the line.

4. The last player races to the front of his Centipede with the balloon, and the passing starts again. So, it's as if the Centipede has taken a step forward. The first Centipede to get all its players across the Finish Line wins.

Balloon Smack

What You Do

1 Players line up single-file against the wall on one side of the room. Players will walk to the opposite wall, so they need a clear path.

2 When the race begins, each player has a balloon and the players begin walking at the same time. For each step taken, a player must smack the balloon up into the air with one or both hands. It's a challenge to match the size of your steps and the power of your hits.

Number of Players: 2 or more
What You Need: 1 balloon per player
Where to Play: in a room
The Point: match your steps and smacks

3 If a balloon touches the ground, the player returns to Start. The first player to reach the opposite wall wins.

Other Ways to Play

Alternate hands: Alternate using right and left hands.

Boot Camp

What You Do

1 Players begin by lying face down on the floor. Everyone needs enough room to move around without knocking into another player.

2 Players count aloud together from one to three, and after "three" they move as fast as they can to do one push-up, one sit-up, and one jumping jack.

3 Players then do two push-ups, two sit-ups, and two jumping jacks. After completing each round, the players add a repetition to each activity. (Three, four, five, and so on.) Players should not wait for others to catch up. (This is a race!)

4 Play until you are tired. The player who does the most rounds of push-ups, sit-ups, and jumping jacks wins. That winning number becomes the number to beat in the next game.

Number of Players: 2 or more
What You Need: nothing
Where to Play: in a carpeted room
The Point: best yourself and your friends

Swim Contest

What You Do

1. One player is the Referee. The other players are Swimmers.

2. Swimmers lay out their rafts on the floor. Swimmers need enough room to dog paddle with their feet and kick their legs without hitting anyone else. The Referee should be able to see all the Swimmers at once.

3. When everyone is ready, the Referee begins the game by blowing the whistle or saying, "On your mark, get set, go!" Swimmers begin swimming, picking up their arms and legs and making swimming motions. (Dog paddle,

Number of Players: 4 or more

What You Need: 1 inflatable raft per player (or beach towels), a whistle (optional)

Where to Play: in a room

The Point: "swim" for the longest time

backstroke, whatever! Swimmers must make sure their arms and legs are not touching the floor.)

4. If a Swimmer touches the floor, the Swimmer is out of the game. The Swimmer who can swim for the longest time wins.

Popcorn Push

What You Do

1 Players make a racecourse that's about 5 feet long and mark Start and Finish lines.

2 Then players line up along the Start Line and kneel at least two feet apart to avoid bumping heads. A kernel of popped corn is placed on the floor in front of each player.

3 At "Go," the players crawl on hands and knees to the Finish Line as they push the popped corn along the floor with their noses.

4 The player who moves a kernel of popped corn across the Finish Line first wins.

Number of Players: 2 or more
What You Need: popcorn, string (optional)
Where to Play: in a room or hallway
The Point: use your nose

Quick Fingers

What You Do

1. Players divide into two teams. Each team gets a length of rope and ties knots in it, letting each player tie a knot. (Players tie any kind of knot.)

2. When both teams are ready, they switch ropes and rush to untie the knots. Each player unties a knot.

3. The first team to untie all the knots from the other team's rope wins.

Number of Players: 6 or more

What You Need: 2 pieces of rope of equal length

Where to Play: anywhere

The Point: race to untie the knots first

Bounce-In

What You Do

1 The players divide into two teams of Bouncers. If there's an extra player, that person can be the Referee who also chases down loose balls.

2 Each team gets one ball and one trash can. They place the trash cans 5 or more feet away and have players stand behind a Bounce Line. Players use a string to mark the line, if necessary.

3 When everyone's ready, a player from each team tries to bounce the ball off the floor and into her goal. Each Bouncer gets three tries to score one point and then rebounds the ball and hands it to the next player.

Number of Players: 4 or more

What You Need: 1 soft rubber ball and 1 short trash can per team, string (optional)

Where to Play: room or hallway with a hard surface

The Point: bounce to score

4 The team with the most points wins.

Other Ways To Play

Time it: Play a one-minute speed round.

Bucket Brigade

What You Do

1 Players divide into two teams. Each team fills a bucket with packing peanuts and grabs a cup and one extra bucket. The teams line up single-file on opposite sides of the room so that the teams are facing one another.

Number of Players: 6 or more
What You Need: 4 buckets, 2 plastic cups, lots of packing peanuts
Where to Play: in a room
The Point: use teamwork to win

2 Each team puts its empty bucket at one end of its line and the full bucket and cup at the other end.

3 Players count aloud from one to three, and after "three" begin the race. Each player nearest a team's full bucket dips the cup in the peanuts and passes the cup down the line to the other end. The last player dumps the contents and passes the empty cup back.

4 The first team to move all its peanuts to the empty bucket wins.

Cup Crossing...

What You Do

1. Players cut two lengths of string about 10 feet long. Players use the pencil to poke a hole in the bottom of each cup, and then thread each length of string through a cup.

2. Players tie each length of string no higher than eye level, side by side (with about two feet between them) across the room. (Players could tie the strings to chairs instead.) The open sides of the cups must face in the same direction.

3. To begin the race, each player lines up at the open side of a cup and blows in the cup to push it along the string, all the way to the other side.

4. The first player to blow a cup to the end wins.

Number of Players: 2

What You Need: string, scissors, tape (optional), pencil, 2 small paper cups, 2 chairs (optional)

Where to Play: in a room

The Point: use your lungpower

Other Ways to Play

Teams: The first player to blow the cup all the way to the other side then slides the cup back to Start and a teammate takes a turn. Or, a player who runs out of breath can ask for help and have a teammate take over.

Bounce, Roll, Toss......

What You Do

1 Players divide into pairs. Each pair is a team. One player from each team stands on each end of the room. One player from each team holds a ball.

2 To play, each team moves the ball across the room and back to the first player from that team. The trick is that on the first cycle the ball must be bounced, on the second cycle the ball is rolled, and on the third cycle the ball is tossed. So, one round of play is made up of "bounce, bounce, roll, roll, toss, toss."

3 The first team to complete five rounds of each cycle wins.

Number of Players: 4 or more
What You Need: 1 small, soft ball per team
Where to Play: in a room
The Point: move the ball

Hand Slap

What You Do

Number of Players: 4 or more
What You Need: nothing
Where to Play: in a room
The Point: send a slap

1. Players divide into two teams. If there is an odd number of players, let one person be the Referee.

2. Each team sits in a single-file row, facing the other team. Agree on one side of the room, to the right or left, to be Start.

3. To play, the player nearest the Start of each team's row (at the end) uses one hand to slap the hand of the next player. (This is a "gimme-5" slap, not a smack.) That player passes it on, down the row, and then back to Start.

4. Pass right-hand slaps in the right hand, and left-hand slaps in the left hand.

5. The first team to send a slap in both directions (down and back up its row) wins.

Other Ways to Play

Backhand: Have players slap the backs of their hands, instead of the palms.

Go behind: Pass the slaps behind the back. Players will have to twist and turn.

Jump, Hop, Skip

What You Do

1 The players divide into two teams. Both teams stand on one side of the room and agree on a Finish Line that lies on the opposite side of the room.

2 When the game begins, a player from each team races to the Finish Line, crosses it, and then returns to Start so the next teammate can complete a lap. Here's the trick: Players must jump, hop on one foot, and then skip—and repeat to get across the room.

3 Teammates help their players keep on track by hollering "jump," "hop," or "skip" at the right time. Players who mess up walk quickly back to Start and begin again.

Number of Players: 4 or more
What You Need: nothing
Where to Play: in a big, carpeted room
The Point: root-on your teammates

4 The first team that completes the circuit wins.

Other Ways to Play

Call out: Have a Referee randomly call out "jump," "hop," or "skip." Players keep moving as directed until they get a new order from the Ref.

Out of Breath

What You Do

1. Players kneel on the floor in a row, all facing the same direction. This is the Start Line.

2. Players pick a spot about 5 feet in front of them and mark a Finish Line using tape.

3. Each player wads up a scrap of paper, making a ball and placing it at the Start Line. The smaller the ball, the easier the game is.

4. When the race begins, players blow on the paper balls, pushing the balls toward the Finish Line.

Number of Players: 2 or more
What You Need: tape (optional), 1 scrap paper per player
Where to Play: in a room
The Point: blow away the competition

5. The first player to finish wins.

Other Ways to Play

Use a straw: Have each player blow through a straw. This will cut down on the amount of spit sprayed on other players.

Didn't-Know-It Poet

What You Do

1. Players line up at one end of the hall-way. The other end is the Finish Line.

2. To begin the game, choose a player to recite and finish the poem "When I was a _____, _____" by creating a rhyme to go with the word chosen for the first blank. For instance, "When I was a kid, you wouldn't believe what I did." That player is now a Poet and begins taking small steps toward the Finish.

3. As quickly as possible, a different player (anyone) must recite the first phrase and create a new rhyming phrase to follow. For instance, "When I was a kid, I called myself Sid." As soon as the final rhyming word is spoken, the first Poet stops moving and the new Poet begins walking.

Number of Players: 3 or more
What You Need: nothing
Where to Play: in a hallway
The Point: out-verse other Poets

4. The new Poet walks until another player (any player) recites a new poem. If a player messes up his rhyme, play continues without any penalties.

5. The first Poet to reach the Finish wins.

Other Ways to Play

Start again: Change the word used to complete "When I was a _____" for each game. Don't start with a word too hard to rhyme with, such as "sausage."

Jump Rope Relay

What You Do

1. The players divide into two teams. Both teams stand on one side of the room. That location is Start. Players agree on a Finish Line that lies on the opposite side of the room.

2. When the race begins, a player from each team jumps rope to the opposite side of the room, turns at the Finish Line, and returns to Start. The next player from each team takes the jump rope and completes the same circuit.

3. The first team to complete the circuit wins.

Number of Players: 4 or more

What You Need: 1 jump rope per team

Where to Play: in a carpeted room without a ceiling fan

The Point: race with a jump rope

Other Ways to Play

Alternate feet: Players alternate which foot they land on with each jump.

Rope twist: Players cross their arms to twist the rope on every other jump.

Spare Change Charge

What You Do

1. Players line up against a wall and put a coin on their foreheads (one coin per player). Players lean their heads back just enough so the coin doesn't fall. (No hands!)

2. To begin the game, players race to the opposite wall, balancing the coins.

3. If a coin falls, that player must stop, pick up the coin, balance it again, and then resume the race.

Number of Players: 2 or more
What You Need: 1 coin per player
Where to Play: in a room
The Point: balance a coin

4. The first player to reach the opposite wall wins.

Slow Down

What You Do

1. Players line up on one side of the room and agree on a Finish Line on the opposite side of the room.

2. One player sets the timer for one minute and says, "Go!" Each player closes both eyes and begins moving as slowly as possible to the Finish Line. Players must be moving constantly.

3. No one can peek at other players or the timer. (If someone peeks, pick a Referee to watch the race, and start from the beginning again.)

Number of Players: 2 or more
What You Need: a timer
Where to Play: in a room
The Point: run a closed-eye race

4. The winner is the last to finish before the timer dings.

Toe-to-Toe

Number of Players: 4 or more
What You Need: stopwatch or watch with a second hand (optional), string (optional)
Where to Play: in a carpeted room
The Point: make the fastest toe-to-toe roll

What You Do

1 Players take off their shoes and socks, and pair up on one side of the room. If there's an extra player, let that person be the Referee.

2 Each pair of players sits on the floor toe to toe. Legs can be bent or straight. The teams line up back to back, so all the teams are in one line.*

3 Agree on a Finish Line on the opposite side of the room. Mark this with a string, if necessary.

4 When the race begins, teams roll any way they want toward the Finish Line. But their toes must touch the whole time. If a pair's toes stop touching, the team has to move back to Start and begin again.

5 The first team to cross the Finish Line—toes still touching—wins.

*If the room is too small to have more than one team race at a time, time each team as it takes a turn rolling to the Finish Line. Compare the results to see who wins.

Other Ways to Play

Hand to hand: Instead of touching toes, try playing the game holding hands.

Hoop Hop

What You Do

1 The players each place a hula hoop against a wall and then line up along the opposite wall.

2 To begin the game, players start hopping toward their hoops as quickly as possible. When they reach their hoops, players hop inside them, slide them up and over, and put the hoop back on the floor.

3 Then the players turn and hop back to Start. The first player to reach Start wins.

Number of Players: 2 or more
What You Need: 1 hula hoop per player
Where to Play: in a room
The Point: move through hoops

Other Ways to Play

Backward: Players hop backward—either throughout the game or just on the race back from the hoop.
Hula: After hopping into the hoops, players must circle the hoops around their waist or hips (by swinging their hips) three times before sliding the hoop up and over.

Hoop Race

What You Do

1 Players divide into two teams. Each team grabs a hula hoop and lines up single-file on opposite sides of the room.

2 The teammates hold hands, and a player on one end of each team's line holds the hoop in a free hand.

3 To begin the race, the teams count aloud together from one to three. After saying "three," each team passes the hoop from one end to the other, without letting go of anyone's hands. (So, players will need to wiggle the hoop over their heads and lift their legs to step through the hoop.)

4 The first team to get the hoop to the free hand of its player on the opposite end of the chain of players wins.

Number of Players: 8 or more
What You Need: 2 hula hoops
Where to Play: in a room
The Point: pass the hoop

BALL GAMES

Who knew you could play
ball in the house?

Bop

What You Do

1 The players stand side by side and link elbows. One player holds a balloon in the hand of the free (unlinked) arm.

2 When the game begins, the players bop the balloon back and forth in the air, using only their free hands.

3 Players count how many passes they complete before the balloon touches the floor.

Number of Players: 2
What You Need: 1 balloon
Where to Play: in a room or hallway
The Point: keep the balloon afloat

500

What You Do

1 One player is the Thrower. The other players are Catchers. The Thrower and Catchers stand on opposite sides of the room.

2 The Thrower tosses the rolled-up sock toward the Catchers and says a number between 50 and 500. That's how many points a Catcher earns for catching it—or loses for trying to catch but missing! (Catchers should call out, "Mine!" to avoid bumping into each other.)

3 The first Catcher to earn 500 points wins and is the new Thrower.

Number of Players: 3 or more
What You Need: rolled-up sock
Where to Play: in a large room
The Point: throw and catch for points

Bocce ....

What You Do

1. Each player takes a paper plate and marks it with initials or a doodle—something to distinguish it from the other plates.

2. A player starts the game by tossing the rolled-up sock to the other end of the room. It doesn't matter where it lands, so long as there is space around it for the paper plates to land.

3. Each player takes a turn tossing his plate at the rolled-up sock. After each player has had a turn, the player whose plate landed on or nearest the sock wins the round and earns a point.

Number of Players: 3 or more

What You Need: rolled-up sock, 1 paper or plastic plate per player

Where to Play: in a room

The Point: make the best toss

4. The first player to earn 11 points wins.

Other Ways to Play

Double up: Give each player 2 plates to toss per turn.

Foot Volleyball

What You Do

1. Players divide the playing area into a volleyball court with two equal-sized sides. They do this by tying the string across the area, about 1 foot above the floor. (It's easiest to use two chairs, one on each side of the court, to create the net.) The string line is the net.

2. Players remove their shoes and divide into two teams, with one team on each side of the net. Players sit on the floor and then lean back onto their hands, lifting up so that only their hands and feet touch the ground, as if crab walking.

3. To start, one team serves the ball by kicking the balloon over the net. If the other team kicks it into or below the net or lets it touch the ground, instead of hitting it back over the net,

Number of Players: 2 or more (even numbers work best)

What You Need: a string or rope, a large inflated balloon

Where to Play: in a room

The Point: use your feet to score

the team that served earns a point and gets to serve again. If the serving team messes up, the other team gets to serve and has a chance to earn points.

4. Play until a team wins by earning 11 points.

Other Ways to Play

Play longer: Agree to play to the score of 15 or 21.

Lower

What You Do

1 Players form a large circle. One player begins the game by tossing the ball to the player on the left. Players continue passing the ball this way around the circle.

2 If a player drops the ball, the others say, "Lower." That player must drop from both feet to both knees, but can still catch and toss the ball. A player on his knees who drops the ball again must drop to his elbows. His next drop means that player has to lie flat on the floor! If a player who has dropped flat on the floor drops the ball again, that player is Out.

Number of Players: 3 or more
What You Need: 1 soft ball
Where to Play: in a room
The Point: stay in the game

3 Play until there's only one person still in the game. That player wins.

Socks of Fury

What You Do

1 Players stand or sit in a wide circle. One player begins the game by calling out another player's name and at the same time quickly tossing the rolled-up sock to that player.

2 The named player must catch the sock and name another player and throw it to that person as quickly as possible. Each name can only be used once.

3 When the sock has gone to each player at least once without anyone dropping it, add the second sock, and then the third.

Number of Players: 6 or more
What You Need: 3 rolled-up socks (preferably socks of different colors)
Where to Play: in a room
The Point: think faster than socks fly

Other Ways to Play

Hustle: Instead of throwing the sock to a player, call the player's name but throw the sock up into the air in the center, so the player has to hustle to catch it.

Round About

What You Do

1 Players sit in a circle facing the center of the circle. One player is the Starter. The Starter begins by passing the ball clockwise.

2 Each player must pass it exactly as the Starter has passed it. For instance, the Starter might pass it by holding it with both hands.

3 After the ball is passed around once, the player to the left of the Starter must pass the ball in a new way. For instance, a player may pass it by balancing it on the back of the hand, or passing it under a leg.

Number of Players: 3 or more

What You Need: a ball of any size

Where to Play: anywhere you can sit in a circle

The Point: pass the ball

4 If a player drops the ball or can't pass it, the player drops out of the circle. Each time a style of passing makes it all the way around the circle, the next person to the left begins a new style of passing.

5 The last remaining player wins. The winner starts the next game.

Pinball

What You Do

1. One player is the pinball Jackpot. The Jackpot stands in the middle of the room. The other players sit on the floor in a circle around the Jackpot. They are the Flippers.

2. The Flippers in the circle spread their legs as wide as is comfortable and touch feet with the players on either side. The area inside the circle of feet is where the Pinball game happens.

3. The Flippers lean forward to rest their hands or arms on the floor. When play starts, the flippers will hit the ball with the hands or arms.

4. The players count aloud together from one to three, and then one of the Flippers starts the ball in play. The Flippers try to hit the Jackpot while he moves around to avoid being hit. The Jackpot can't leave the circle and the ball can't leave the floor.

5. The Flipper who hits the Jackpot with the ball becomes the new Jackpot.

Number of Players: 5 or more
What You Need: a soft ball
Where to Play: on a floor
The Point: hit the Jackpot

Bowling Bridges

What You Do

1 Players divide into two teams. The teams line up on opposite sides of the room so teammates stand side by side and face the other team. Teammates stand no less than 1 foot apart and with their feet spread no less than the width of the ball.

2 To play, teams take turns rolling the ball at one another. Players aren't allowed to move while a ball is being rolled. If the ball goes between the legs of a player, that player is out of the game.

Number of Players: 6 or more
What You Need: 1 small ball
Where to Play: in a room
The Point: eliminate opponents

3 The first team to eliminate everyone on the other team wins.

Broom Hockey

What You Do

1. Players divide into two teams. Each player needs a broom. Each team needs a scoring goal, and the goals should be located at opposite ends of the room. (A hand towel makes a good goal.)

2. Teams line up in the middle of the room. Players from each team should have their backs to the goal they're protecting and be facing their scoring goal. One rolled-up sock is the Puck.

3. To begin, a player tosses the Puck straight up into the air. When it hits the floor, players begin trying to push the Puck to their goal to score a point.

Number of Players: 2 or more

What You Need: 1 rolled-up sock, 1 broom per player, 2 hand towels (optional)

Where to Play: on a hard floor

The Point: score goals

4. After a team scores, the other team gets a "free" chance to sweep the Puck to a teammate or toward their scoring goal. (But the other team can block or intercept.)

5. The first team to score 11 points wins.

Golf Ball Billiards

What You Do

1. Players make a circle on the floor with the string. The circle should be 3 feet in diameter. Players place nine golf balls inside the circle.

2. Players use a colored golf ball (or mark a plain one) for the cue ball. Each player gets a pencil and decides in which order to play.

3. Players use the eraser-end of the pencil like a real pool cue, sliding it along the hand to push the cue ball into a golf ball.

4. The goal is to knock as many golf balls out of the circle as possible. If a player knocks a ball out, he gets another turn, unless the cue ball is knocked out as well. A player can shoot until failing to knock a ball out of the circle.

Number of Players: 2 or more

What You Need: string, 10 golf balls, and 1 unsharpened pencil per player

Where to Play: on a hard floor

The Point: score 5 knock-outs

5. Then the next player shoots. The player shoots from wherever the cue ball rolled at the end of the last player's turn. If the ball goes out of the circle, the next player can put it anywhere in the circle.

6. Whoever knocks five balls out of the circle first wins.

Other Ways to Play

One at a time: Take turns every time, regardless of whether a player knocked a ball out of the circle.

More fun than 52-Pickup. Guaranteed!

Anxiety

Number of Players: 2 or more
What You Need: deck of cards
Where to Play: anywhere
The Point: tickle or be tickled, hug or be hugged, remove shoes or have your shoes removed

What You Do

1   Players sit in a circle. One player deals cards one at a time to each player until all the cards are dealt.

2   Players all flip over one card at the same time and toss it in the middle of the circle. If anyone flips over the Ace of Spades, all the other players tickle that player. The Jack of Hearts means the player gets bear hugs. The 3 of Diamonds means the player's shoes are quickly removed by the other players.

3   If no one flips over one of the cards described above, keep playing until someone does. The longer the game lasts, the more anxious the players become. The game is over when each of those three cards have been played.

Even Steven

What You Do

1 One player is the Dealer and deals seven cards to each player.

2 The Dealer places the rest of the deck face down on the table.

3 The opponent begins the game by placing one card face up on the table. This will be the Pile.

4 The Dealer must play a single card of the same value as the card laid in the Pile. This matching card is called an Even Steven.

5 If the Dealer has no Even Steven, the Dealer can't play any card. He must pick up a card from the deck. Next,

Number of Players: 2
What You Need: deck of cards
Where to Play: on a table or floor
The Point: get rid of your cards

it's the opponent's turn. Whenever a player fails to lay out an Even Steven, the player must pick up one card from the deck, and the other player may lay out any new card face up on the Pile.

6 If the Dealer has an Even Steven and lays it down, it's now the opponent's turn to lay down another Even Steven, or pick up a card from the deck.

7 The first player to use up all the cards in his hand wins.

Guess What

What You Do

1. One player is the Dealer and deals five cards to each player. Players hold the five cards in their hands so no one else can see them.

2. The Dealer takes the top card from the deck and places that card face down in front of the players. That card is the What.

3. Each player guesses which card What is, and then "bids" a card from her hand based on that guess. To bid, a player places just one of her cards face up above or below the face-down card. Place a card above to say you think your card is of greater value. Place a card below to say it is of lesser value than the face-down card.

Number of Players: 2 or more
What You Need: deck of cards
Where to Play: on a table or floor
The Point: guess and bid

4. When every player has made one bid, the Dealer turns over the What to reveal it. The Dealer determines who won their bid. Those players get to take their Winning Card and set it aside as one point. Players who lost their bids lose those cards; the cards go to the bottom of the deck along with the What.

5. For each round, the Dealer places a new What face down and players bid one card. When five rounds have been played, the player with the most points wins.

Hat Trick

What You Do

1 Players divide the cards equally among themselves and set the hat upside down on the floor against the wall.

2 Players agree on a Toss Line and take turns flipping the cards against the wall, standing, sitting, or squatting behind the Toss Line.

3 A player earns one point for each successful bank shot. No points are earned for tossing the card directly into the hat. Scoring three times in a row is a Hat Trick; that player earns three extra points.

Number of Players: 2 or more
What You Need: cards, hat
Where to Play: against a wall
The Point: score bank shots with cards

4 After all the cards are tossed, the player with the most points wins.

Other Ways to Play

Three-point shots: Create a second Toss Line, further away, from which players can make three-point shots.

Lightning Pairs

What You Do

1. One player deals a card to each player, clockwise, until all the cards are handed out.

2. Play begins immediately, as players hold the cards in their hands and sort out all the pairs. Pairs are laid face up on the table, according to the following rule: only one kind of pair can be laid out. So, the first player to lay out a pair of 2s is the only player who can lay out a pair of 2s, etc. Be quick!

3. After players lay out the allowed pairs, the player to the left of the Dealer pulls one card (any card) from the hand of any one of the players. If that card makes an original pair with a card in the player's hand, the player lays the pair on the table.

Number of Players: 2 or more
What You Need: deck of cards
Where to Play: on a table or floor
The Point: collect the most pairs to earn points

4. Play continues once around the table, with each player getting just one chance to pick a card per turn.

5. At the end of a round, the player with the most pairs earns a point. Play until someone has earned 10 points.

Crazy 8s

What You Do

1 One player is the Dealer and deals seven cards to each player. Players hold the cards in their hands.

2 The Dealer stacks the rest of the deck face down in the middle of the table. The Dealer then turns over the top card from the deck and sets it beside the deck, creating a Discard pile.

3 The first player to the left of the Dealer starts. The aim is to discard one card per turn. But the discarded card must be the same as the face-up card, either in value (9, Jack) or suit (Heart, Spade, Diamond, Club).

Number of Players: 2 or more
What You Need: deck of cards
Where to Play: on a table or floor
The Point: empty your hand

4 If the player does not have a card to discard, the player draws one card from the deck. If that card cannot be discarded, the player keeps it, and the next player has a turn.

5 Eights are wild, so a player could discard an 8 on a turn, no matter the value or suit of the face-up card. The player who discards all cards first wins.

House of Cards

Number of Players: 2 or more
What You Need: cards
Where to Play: on a table or floor
The Point: construct a House of Cards

What You Do

1   One player starts the game by trying to build a structure at the center of the table using no more than four cards.

2   Players take turns using two to four cards to add onto the structure.

3   The player who knocks down the House of Cards has to clean up the cards and starts the new House.

Quadruplets

What You Do

1 One player deals a face-down card to each player, clockwise, until all the cards are handed out.

2 Players look at their cards, but don't show them to anyone. Players lay their cards face down on the table.

3 Players want to collect as many sets of four of a kind as they can. When a player has four of a kind, the player turns them face up.

4 Taking turns and moving clockwise, each player asks any one of the other players for exactly the card wanted. (If a player has an Ace, that player will want all the Aces, but can only ask for one at a time at each turn, such as the Ace of Hearts.)

Number of Players: 2 or more
What You Need: deck of cards
Where to Play: tabletop or flat surface
The Point: reunite each set of quadruplets

5 If the player asked has the card, that player has to hand it over. Then the next player takes a turn.

6 Players must remember to turn over any four of a kind collection as soon as possible. Any face-down cards are fair game for other players to request.

7 The game ends when all of the quadruplets have been reunited and no one has any cards left. If you want to pick a winner, let the winner be the player who has collected the most sets of four.

Matches

What You Do

1. One player is the Dealer and deals eight cards to the center of the table, placing them face up. Then the Dealer deals four cards, face down, to each player. The extra cards are set aside, face down.

2. Players look at their cards, and then turn them face up. The player to the left of the Dealer begins play.

3. On each turn a player can remove a card from the center, but only if one of her cards matches it in suit or value. For instance, if there's a 5 of Clubs in the center, a player holding any Club or any 5 could pick the 5 of Clubs as a match. The player who removes a card pairs it with the "match" and lays them in a pile. A player who can't make a match must put a card in the center of the table. Play continues to the left.

4. When all players have used or handed out their cards, the player with the most matches wins.

Number of Players: 2 or more
What You Need: deck of cards
Where to Play: on a table or floor
The Point: make the most matches

Trap

Number of Players: 3 to 6
What You Need: deck of cards
Where to Play: on a table or floor
The Point: trap your opponents

What You Do

1. The Dealer distributes an even number of cards face down to the players. If there are any extra cards, set them aside face down. Players can look at their cards.

2. The player to the left of the Dealer lays out one card face up. Any card.

3. The next player to the left can Trap the card by placing the next lower and higher cards on either side. To trap a 6, for instance, a player would need to surround it with a 5 and a 7. After trapping a card, the Trapper scoops up all three cards and stacks them nearby. This stack counts as one point.

4. If the player can't Trap the card, the player must lay out another card else-where on the table. Play continues moving clockwise, and players can play off of any cards on the table. That means players can Trap their own cards.

5. When all the cards have been laid on the table once, the player with the most points wins.

Royalty

What You Do

1. One player deals a card to each player until all the cards are handed out. Players can't look at their cards.

2. The player to the left of the Dealer quickly lays out one card face up, creating a pile. The next player lays a card on the pile and so on, so each player in turn is quickly laying out a card one at a time.

3. As soon as anyone sees a royalty card (King, Queen, or Jack), the first player to act out the royal character gets the royalty card and all the cards under it. Winning a King requires that a player be the first to say, "The King says it is so, and so it is so." Winning a Queen requires that the player be the first

Number of Players: 2 or more
What You Need: deck of cards
Where to Play: on a table or floor
The Point: act out characters

to kiss the air to the right and left, as if kissing each cheek of a friend. A player must be the first to stand and salute in order to win a Jack. If you have trouble noticing who is the first to correctly complete any of these actions, assign a Referee.

4. That winning player puts the pile of cards in her hand and starts a new pile, laying down the first card.

5. The player who has all the cards at game's end wins.

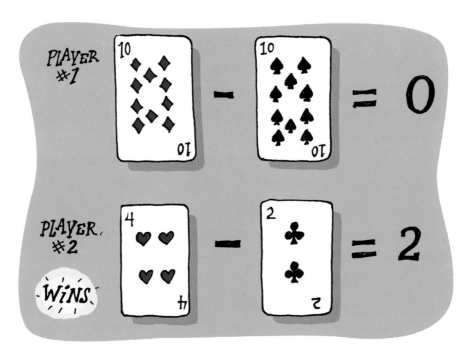

Subtraction War

What You Do

1. One player deals a card to each player until all the cards are handed out. Players can't look at their cards.

2. To begin the game, all players lay out two cards, face up, at the same time. Players subtract their own lower card from their higher card. (Every face card—king, queen, jack—and aces are worth 10 points.) The player with the highest difference wins the round and takes all the cards played.

3. The player who has all the cards at game's end wins.

Number of Players: 2 or more
What You Need: deck of cards
Where to Play: on a table or floor
The Point: use subtraction to win cards

Triplet......

What You Do

1 The Dealer distributes an even number of cards to the players. If there are any extra cards, the Dealer sets them aside, face down.

2 After looking at her cards, the player to the left of the Dealer turns one of her cards face up.

3 The next player to the left (moving clockwise) can create a Triplet using the face-up card. To do this, he needs to use two cards of the same value or suit from his hand. So, there could be a Triplet made up of diamonds, or a Triplet made up of kings or fours, etc. The Triplet is laid face up.

Number of Players: 3 or more
What You Need: deck of cards
Where to Play: on a table or floor
The Point: empty your hand of cards

4 If that player can't make a Triplet, he must turn one of his cards face up.

5 Play continues moving clockwise, with each player either making a Triplet from any face-up card or laying down a card.

6 The first player to use all the cards in her hand wins.

TRIPLETS

MARBLES, COINS & STONES

Shoot, flip, and toss.

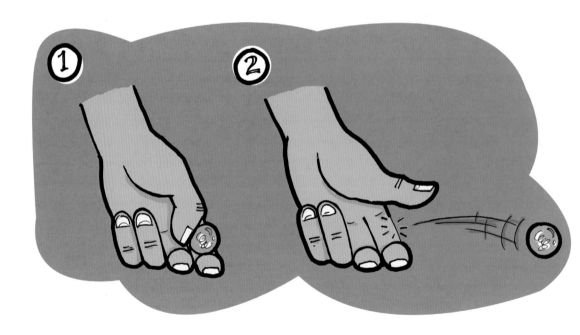

Basic Marbles

What You Do

1 Players make a circle on the floor with the dental floss. It should be about 2 to 3 feet wide. Players choose an order for playing (youngest goes first, or play moves clockwise, etc.).

2 Each player puts the same number of marbles into the center of the circle, saving one marble each to use as a shooter marble. The shooter marble works best if it is larger and heavier than the other marbles. (Players use shooter marbles to knock the other marbles out of the circle.)

3 To play, a player places his shooter marble outside of the circle, holds it as shown in the illustration, and flicks it toward the other marbles.

Number of Players: 2 or more

What You Need: dental floss or very thin string, marbles

Where to Play: on a hard floor

The Point: knock marbles out of the circle

4 A player keeps any marbles knocked out of the circle. The player continues to shoot until failing to knock out any marbles. The player leaves the shooter marble where it is, unless it rolled outside of the circle.

5 If a player hits another player's shooter marble, then he gets all the marbles the other player has collected.

6 After all the marbles have been knocked out of the circle, the player with the most marbles wins.

Double Ring

What You Do

Number of Players: 2 or more

1. Players draw a circle on the floor with the dental floss. It should be about 2 to 3 feet wide. Players draw another, smaller circle inside that circle. The smaller circle should be about 6 inches across.

Number of Players: 2 or more

What You Need: dental floss or very thin string, marbles

Where to Play: on a hard floor

The Point: stay in the right circles

2. Players each grab one marble to use as a shooter marble, and then place all the other marbles in the inner circle. (Larger, heavier marbles make better shooter marbles.) To begin play, players take turns making one shot from inside the outer circle, aiming to knock the marbles out of the inner circle. (To shoot the marble, you can hold it as shown in the illustration on page 142.)

3. A player keeps the marbles she knocks out. If her shooter marble stops in the inner circle, she must forfeit those marbles and put them back in the inner circle. She picks up her shooter marble and it's the next player's turn.

4. When all the marbles are gone from the inner circle, the player with the most marbles wins.

Bull's Eye

What You Do

1 Players make a 1-foot wide circle on the floor with the dental floss. Players put one marble into the center of the circle for each player.

2 Players take turns standing over the circle and dropping a new marble into it. Players must drop the marble from their eye level.

3 If a player's marble knocks any marbles out of the ring, that player gets to keep them, including the dropped marble. But players must leave any marbles that remain in the ring, including the dropped marble. (Players use a new marble for every turn.)

Number of Players: 2 or more
What You Need: dental floss or very thin string, marbles
Where to Play: on a hard floor
The Point: make bomber shots

4 When all the marbles have been knocked out of the circle, players count their marbles. The player with the most marbles wins.

Fivestones

What You Do

Number of Players: 2 or more
What You Need: 5 stones (or dried beans)
Where to Play: anywhere you can sit in a circle on the floor
The Point: catch as many stones as possible

1 One player starts by tossing five stones into the air with one hand. The player tries to catch them on the back of that same hand. If the player doesn't catch any of the stones on the back of his hand, it's the next player's turn.

2 If the player catches any of the stones, his turn continues and he throws those "caught" stones into the air from the back of his hand. He must try to catch them in the palm of the same hand. If he doesn't catch any, it's the next player's turn. (Each new turn begins with step 1 and all five stones in play.)

3 If he succeeds in catching any of the stones in his palm, his turn continues and he has the chance to earn points. If he caught only one, he must repeat step 2. If he succeeds, he gets a point and it's the next player's turn. (Each new turn begins with step 1 and all five stones in play.)

4 If he succeeded in catching more than one stone in step 2, he can try to earn a point for each stone. To do this, he keeps one stone in the throwing hand and tosses the other stones on the floor. Now he must toss the single stone into the air, pick up at least one stone from the floor, and catch the thrown stone—all in one motion with the same hand. If he can't, it's the next player's turn. (Each new turn begins with step 1 and all five stones in play.)

5 If he succeeds, he earns a point for each stone he picked up. He can try again to pick up each of the remaining stones, but the first time he fails, it's the next player's turn. (Each new turn begins with step 1 and all five stones in play.)

6 After everyone has had a turn, the player who earned the most points during his turn wins.

Pyramid Marbles

Number of Players: 2 or more
What You Need: dental floss and marbles
Where to Play: on a hard floor
The Point: bust the pyramid

What You Do

1. Players make a small circle, about 1 foot in diameter, on the hard floor using the dental floss. Players decide in which order they'll shoot and agree on how many rounds to play. Each player should also choose a shooter marble to use during the game.

2. The first player builds a pyramid of marbles in the middle of the circle by placing three marbles next to each other in a triangle shape and placing a fourth marble on top.

3. The next player flicks his shooter marble at the base of the pyramid. The player gets to keep any marbles that are knocked out of the circle and set them aside as points. Then he builds a new pyramid with new and leftover marbles. It's the next player's turn.

4. Play continues until all the marbles are claimed and set aside as points. (The pyramid will be smaller as more marbles are taken out of the game.) The player with the most marbles at the end of the game wins.

Shoot 'Em

Number of Players: 2 or more
What You Need: marbles
Where to Play: on a hard floor
The Point: hit marbles for points

What You Do

1. Each player selects a shooter marble to set aside and use throughout the game. (A shooter marble works best when it is larger and heavier than the other marbles in play.)

2. Players set up a straight line of marbles. The marbles should be spaced so that two marbles can pass between them. Then players agree on the location of a Shooting Line at least 1 foot from the row of marbles.

3. To begin the game, a player kneels at the Shooting Line and flicks his shooter marble at the row of marbles. (Check out the technique shown in the illustration on page 142.) The player gets just one flick per turn. If his marble strikes any of the marbles in the row, he picks them up as points.

4. The player leaves his shooter marble where it landed. It's the next player's turn. She can earn points the same way. But, anyone who hits another player's shooter marble with her own shooter or with a stray marble loses an earned point and has to add a marble to the line of marbles.

5. Players continue taking turns, shooting from wherever their shooter marbles came to rest.

6. When all the marbles are gone, the player with the most marbles in hand is the winner.

Monkey Feet

Number of Players: 2 or more
What You Need: 1 coin per player (use the same kind of coin for everyone)
Where to Play: in a room
The Point: use your feet like hands

What You Do

1. Players remove their socks and shoes and stand on one side of the room. They must agree on an imaginary Start Line on that side of the room, and an imaginary Finish Line on the opposite side of the room. (Real lines marked with string could interfere with the game.)

2. Each barefoot player gets one coin and lays it on the floor. Players count down from three to start the game. Then each player must pick up the coin using only one foot, and move the coin to the Finish Line.

3. Ways to pick up a coin include pressing into the coin with the fleshy ball of the foot (this is easiest to do on hard floors) and grabbing the coin between two toes (this is easiest to do on carpeted floors).

4. Players can drop coins and pick them up again, but if the coin rolls forward it must be taken back (by hand) to where the player's foot was when the coin dropped. Then the player continues toward the Finish Line.

5. The first player to reach the Finish Line with a coin "in foot" wins.

Other Ways to Play

More monkeying: All players sit on the floor. Instead of picking up a coin with one foot, players pick up and carry the coin between both feet, scooting along the floor by alternating between lifting their rear ends and pushing with their hands.

Shuffleboard

Number of Players: 2 or more

What You Need: 4 coins per player (it's best if everyone has the same kinds of coins), tape, a pencil with an eraser (or one per player)

Where to Play: on a table or floor

The Point: score points with good slides

What You Do

1. Players mark off a scoring area with tape at one end of the table. The scoring area should have four sections: a 10-point area nearest the edge of the table, a 7-point area farther from the edge, an 8-point area even farther from the edge, and a minus 10-point penalty area near the middle of the table.

2. Each player gets four coins and lays them at the opposite end of the table. Players can mark or agree on where to put a Start Line.

3. To begin the game, a player uses the eraser-end of a pencil to slide one coin at a time toward the scoring area. The eraser should not pass the Start Line. Players can bump their own coins, and gain or lose points depending on how the coin moves, or knock a coin off the table. Players keep their own scores.

4. After sliding each of the four coins, the first player adds up the points earned (or lost) and collects the coins. Each player gets a turn.

5. The player with the most points wins.

PEN & PAPER GAMES

Word play, guessing games, and more.

A Hit or Miss

What You Do

1 Players each make two grids, using one piece of paper per grid. One grid is the Top Secret Map; the other is the Sea Map. Don't peek at the other player's maps! Each grid needs 10 rows and 10 columns. Players label the rows 1 through 10 and label the columns A through J.

2 Each player draws four ships on the Top Secret Map, using these guidelines: one ship covers four grid squares, one ship covers three grid squares, and two ships cover two grid squares each. The ships cannot overlap, but they can be horizontal or vertical.

3 Players turn their Top Secret Maps over so the opponent can't see them.

Number of Players: 2
What You Need: 2 pencils, 4 sheets of paper
Where to Play: anywhere
The Point: sink your opponent's ships

4 The game begins when one player (the "Caller") launches a rocket to a location on the opponent's grid. For instance, "E, 7" is a location. The Caller marks that location on his Sea Map. The opponent has to say if that was a "Hit" or a "Miss."

5 Players take turns launching rockets and tracking the hits and misses. The first player to sink all of the opponent's ships wins.

Pals

Number of Players: 3 or more
What You Need: pens, paper, hat
Where to Play: anywhere
The Point: guess what your friends think

What You Do

1. Every player gets a piece of paper, a scrap of paper, and a pen. On the scrap of paper, each player writes one question that any player might answer during the game. Write questions such as, "What's your favorite book?" or "If you were an animal that lived in the sea, what animal would you be?"

2. Players fold up the scraps of paper and put them all in the hat. They then divide into two teams.

3. The teams take turns having one player be the Pal who draws a scrap from the hat. The Pal reads it aloud and writes down the answer on his paper while his teammates each write down the answer they think he will give (on their papers). Teammmates should not peek at each other's responses.

4. When everyone is ready, the Pal asks his teammates to read what they wrote, one at a time. The teammate then reads his answer and gives his team one point for every correct answer they had. The next team takes a turn beginning at step 3.

5. When all of the questions have been answered, the team with the most points wins.

Slermcabs

Number of Players: 2 or more

What You Need: 1 sheet of paper and 1 pencil per player

Where to Play: on a table or floor

The Point: find hidden words

What You Do

1 Each player writes down five Slermcabs on a page. (Slermcabs are anagrams, which are words whose letters are scrambled. For instance, "erapp" is an anagram for "paper," "xdime" is an anagram for "mixed," and "slermcabs" is an anagram for "scrambles.") To make play easier, limit each Slermcab to 5 letters.

2 After each player has written down five Slermcabs, players swap pages.

3 Beginning at the same time, players try to unscramble the words on their pages. The first player to solve all five Slermcabs wins.

4 It's okay for a player to solve an anagram by finding a word that's different from what the player who wrote it was thinking. (But all the letters must be used to create the word.)

Bingo

Number of Players: 3 or more

What You Need: 1 piece of paper per player, pens, lots of coins or buttons, 60 small scraps of paper, bowl or basket

Where to Play: in a room

The Point: mark 5 in a row

What You Do

1 One player is the Caller. The Caller writes a number between 1 and 30 on each scrap, using each number twice. Then the Caller marks 12 scraps each with a "B," an "I," an "N," a "G," and an "O." There will be 60 scraps total, and each will have a number and a letter. (B1, G29, etc.)

2 The other players make Bingo sheets. Each sheet needs a grid with five rows and five columns, for a total of 25 squares. Players write B-I-N-G-O across the top, so that one letter is above each column. Players write "free" in the center square.

3 Players write a number between 1 and 30 in each empty square. No number may be repeated. Each grid should be unique. (No peeking at other grids.)

4 The Caller puts the scraps of paper in a large bowl. Then each player grabs a couple handfuls of coins and places one coin in the "free" square.

5 The game begins when the Caller closes both eyes, reaches into the bowl, and pulls out a scrap. The Caller opens her eyes and calls out the letter and number on the scrap, such as "G 21." Any player who has that combination on his grid places a coin in that square. The Caller sets the used scrap aside and continues selecting and announcing numbers.

6 Players want their grids to spell "BINGO" by having coins lined up horizontally, vertically, or diagonally, one coin or mark under each letter.

Any player who gets a BINGO must be the first to yell, "BINGO!" The Caller decides who yelled first, and then checks the player's grid against the letters and numbers on the used scraps. If the player was mistaken and does not have BINGO, play continues.

7 The player who spells BINGO first is the winner and becomes the new Caller. Players clear their grids of coins to begin a new game. All the scraps go back into the bowl.

Call-Out Crosswords

Number of Players: 2 or more

What You Need: 1 pen and 1 piece of paper per player, a timer or watch

Where to Play: anywhere

The Point: earn points for words

What You Do

1. Each player draws a grid on a piece of paper, using five squares across and five squares down, for a total of 25 squares.

2. One player starts the game by saying a letter, any letter. Every other letter must be a vowel, until the vowels are all used. The players each write that letter in any square. Players should be trying to think of words that can be read forward or backward in the grid, across, down, or diagonally. Players should place each letter in a strategic location that will allow it to be used in several words on the grid.

3. Players take turns calling out a letter until 12 squares are filled. Then the players take a few minutes to add any letters they choose to try to spell more words. (Players should agree on a time limit of two to four minutes.)

4. When time is up, players give themselves two points for every two-letter word, three points for every three-letter word, and so on. The player with the highest score wins.

Other Ways To Play

Harder: Take turns calling out letters until 15, 18, or 20 squares are filled.

No or Yes

Number of Players: 4 or more
What You Need: 2 pieces of paper per player, a pen
Where to Play: in a room
The Point: answer, but don't speak

What You Do

1 One player is the Talker. The Talker stands on one side of the room. Players line up side-by-side on the other side of the room.

2 Only the Talker can speak. Players can't speak. Players grab two pieces of paper each and use the pen to write "no" on one and "yes" on the other. To answer, players will hold up one of these signs.

3 When the players are ready, the Talker starts the game by asking a question and asking the players to answer yes or no. The Talker should stick to things that are clearly yes or no questions. The Talker must also know the correct answer to his questions. The Talker could ask anything from "Is my birthday in February?" to "Is a salamander a fish?"

4 When every player has answered, the Talker reveals the answer. For each correct answer a player takes a step toward the Talker. (A player can challenge the Talker, if she thinks his answer was wrong. The player has five minutes to look it up in a reference book, or on the Internet, with a parent's permission. If the player is correct, she gets to take two steps. There is no penalty for the Talker. Then play continues.)

5 The first player to reach the Talker becomes the new Talker.

Celebrity

What You Do

1. Each player gets five scraps of paper. On three of the scraps each player can write the name of someone famous (a Major Celebrity). On two scraps, each player must write the name of someone not in the room who is personally known by at least one other person in the room (a Little-Known Celebrity).

2. The players put the names into the hat. One of the players starts the timer. The player draws a name from the hat one at a time and has one minute to get the rest of the players to guess the names of as many Celebrities as possible. As that player describes the Celebrity, he can't use any names of people or places. The player also can't skip any names but must use the name he drew from the hat.

Number of Players: 4 or more
What You Need: scraps of paper, pencils, hat, and a timer
Where to Play: anywhere
The Point: get players to guess who

3. Anyone who guesses correctly gets the scrap of paper as a point and takes the next turn. If the first player didn't succeed in making the others guess the name within the time limit, that name remains a mystery and goes back into the hat. If no one won the point, play moves clockwise.

4. Play until all the Celebrities have been named. The player with the most scraps of paper wins.

Act Out

Number of Players: 3 or more
What You Need: scrap paper, pencils, and a hat or paper bag
Where to Play: anywhere
The Point: act out or guess words

What You Do

1 Players each grab three scraps of paper and write one word that names a person or thing (a noun) on each scrap. A player then puts the papers into the hat.

2 A player starts the game by picking a piece of paper from the hat and acting out that word. She can't speak, make sounds, or use any objects to help her act out the word.

3 The other players try to guess the word. The player who guesses correctly takes the next turn choosing and acting out a word.

4 Play continues until all the words are used. The person with the most correct guesses wins.

Super Sketch

What You Do

1. Fold the paper into quarters in an accordion-style fold. Do this by folding down one-fourth of the length of the paper from the top of the page, then folding that section to the back side of the paper to create the second fold, and then folding those parts toward the front of the page. You will create three folds and four sections of equal size.

2. Players will sketch an original superhero in four parts, one player at a time. The parts are: the head and neck area (on the top section); the torso and arms area (on the second section); the lower body area to the knees (on the third section); and the lower leg and feet area (on the fourth section). Players can't talk about what they'll draw or look at anyone else's sketch until the end of the game.

Number of Players: up to 4
What You Need: sheet of paper, colored pens or pencils
Where to Play: on a smooth, flat surface
The Point: draw a hilarious picture

3. As the other players close their eyes, one player begins drawing on the uppermost fold of the paper. This player is the Drawer.

4. The Drawer folds the drawn portion back, so it can't be seen, and passes the paper to the next player. Again, everyone except the new Drawer closes both eyes.

5. Players pass the picture until everyone has drawn a section.

6. Now the players open their eyes, unfold the paper, and see what superhero they created.

Memory

What You Do

1. One player is the Tester. The Tester collects 10 objects and places them in the bag so the players can't see them. While the other players are looking away, the Tester puts the objects on the floor and covers them with the towel.

2. When everyone is ready, the Tester uncovers the objects and silently counts to 15. The players should look at the objects and memorize what's there. Then the Tester covers the objects with the towel again.

3. The players write down the objects they saw. (The Tester decides how much time to give the players, and must announce the time limit when he covers the objects.)

Number of Players: 3 or more

What You Need: 10 objects, a bag to hold the objects, a towel, 1 pen per player, and 1 piece of paper per player

Where to Play: in a room

The Point: test your memory

4. When time is up, the Tester uncovers the objects and the players compare their lists. Players earn one point for each object they remembered. The player with the most points is the next Tester. (If there's a tie, everyone with the highest number of points wins.)

Other Ways to Play

When?: Give the players more or less time to memorize, to make the game harder or easier.

What?: Give the players more or fewer objects to memorize.

Where?: Give players an extra point for remembering the location of each object. (One point per object.)

Picture This

What You Do

1 Players divide into two teams. Each team needs several pieces of paper and a pen.

2 Each team picks a player to be their first Artist. To choose what to draw, an Artist from either team puts a finger on any page in the book. Both Artists look at the words nearest the finger, without showing anyone else. The nearest noun or verb is what both will draw. (The Artists can tell the players if it is a noun or verb.)

3 The players count aloud together from one to three. After saying "three," both Artists close their eyes and begin drawing. Artists can't write any words or speak. Teammates try to guess what is being drawn by their Artist. No peeking at the other team's work!

Number of Players: 6 or more
What You Need: 2 pen, paper, book
Where to Play: on a table
The Point: make sense of a blind sketch

4 An Artist tells the team when it's guessed correctly. The first team to figure out the word based on their Artist's drawing wins.

5 It's fun to look at the drawings again after everyone knows what the Artists were trying to draw. Play several times so everyone gets to be an Artist.

ODDBALLS

Games that are too much fun to classify.

Bodyguard

What You Do

1. One player is the Bodyguard. The Bodyguard stands in the middle of the room and sets the soda bottle nearby. The soda bottle is the Client. (The Bodyguard can name the Client after someone famous.)

Number of Players: 4 or more

What You Need: soda bottle half filled with water and tightly closed, a soft rubber ball

Where to Play: in a room

The Point: protect the Client

2. The other players are the Fanatics. They sit in a circle at least 3 feet from the Client and try to roll the ball into it. The Bodyguard tries to protect the Client by blocking the ball with any body part. The Bodyguard can't touch the Client.

3. Fanatics rebound the ball and re-roll it as quickly as possible. If a Fanatic knocks over the Client, that Fanatic becomes the new Bodyguard.

Capture the Flag

Number of Players: 6 or more

What You Need: 2 different flags or 2 different t-shirts

Where to Play: in a house

The Point: steal your opponent's flag

What You Do

1 Players divide into two teams, and divide the play area into two territories. One team controls each territory, and the more area between the territories, the better. (So, one team could have the living room and the other could have a bedroom that's down the hall from the living room.)

2 To begin the game, each team has a Flag and hides it in its territory. Both teams can send Spies to watch the other team, but both teams can also post Lookouts to warn teammates about the Spies. Walking fast is expected, but no running is allowed. (You're in the house, remember?)

3 When both teams have hidden their Flags, they announce it and the game begins: each team tries to find and capture the other's Flag and bring it to their territory. An opponent tagged in enemy territory must sit there and can only be freed by the touch of a teammate. If a player is caught running, that player must also sit and wait to be freed. (If you have disputes about who is tagged or who isn't obeying the rules, assign a Referee.)

4 The first team to capture the opponent's Flag and take it to their territory wins.

Could Be

What You Do

1 One player is the Collector and collects various items that are hard to identify by feel alone. (How about a small jar of lip gloss, a single piece of unwrapped candy, or a scoop of ice cream in a sealed plastic bag?) The Collector puts each item into the bag.

2 The players sit in a circle. The Collector hands the bag to a player and the player tries to figure out what is in the bag just by reaching inside and feeling each item. Each player can make one guess per turn. If he's correct, he takes the item out of the bag, and then passes the bag to the next player.

Number of Players: 4 or more
What You Need: various items, 1 paper bag
Where to Play: anywhere
The Point: identify items by touch

3 After all the items are named, the player with the most correct guesses wins.

All Thumbs

Number of Players: 3 or more

What You Need: chocolate bar, wrapping paper, tape, oven mitts, pair of dice

Where to Play: anywhere

The Point: unwrap the present

What You Do

1 Wrap the chocolate bar in wrapping paper, on top of the original packaging. Wrap it several times, so that the bar is completely covered at least three times. It is the Present.

2 Players sit in a circle. Put the Present in the middle, along with the oven mitts.

3 To begin the game, players take turns rolling the dice. (One roll per player per round.) If the dice add up to five, that player quickly puts on the mitts and tries to open the Present.

4 The other players continue rolling the dice as quickly as possible. As soon as another player's roll adds up to five, the first player must immediately stop trying to open the Present. The player who had a winning roll puts on the mitts and tries to open the Present.

5 The first player to completely unwrap the Present—including the original packaging—wins. He should share it with all the players.

Flashlight Tag

What You Do

1 One player is IT. IT decides on the theme, such as "actors" or "books," and tells the players.

2 IT stands in the middle of the dark room holding the flashlight. IT closes both eyes. The other players spread out in the room, but can't hide behind anything.

3 IT counts aloud from one to three, and after "three" the players begin moving quietly around the room. At any time IT can open both eyes and shine the flashlight on a player. The player must immediately yell the name of an actor (or whatever fits the theme). If he pauses at all before replying, he's Out of the game.

4 If the player survives, IT closes both eyes and the game continues. The last player in the game wins and becomes the new IT.

Number of Players: 5 or more
What You Need: a flashlight
Where to Play: in a dark room
The Point: yell out a correct answer

Hackeysack

Number of Players: 2 or more
What You Need: hackeysack or jianzi
Where to Play: in a room
The Point: get the most Hacks

What You Do

1. Players take turns bouncing the hack-eysack off any body part. Players might use their hands, feet, knees, head, etc., to keep it in the air for as long as possible.

2. A hit is a Hack, and all players count the Hacks aloud. A player's turn ends when the hackeysack hits the floor, a wall, or anything other than the player.

3. After everyone has had a turn, the player with the most Hacks wins.

Make a Jianzi

A jianzi is a Chinese shuttlecock that you can use like a hackeysack. Make a jianzi with two quarters, a large paper napkin, and a little bit of string. Put two quarters in the center of the napkin. Fold the edges of the napkin up and twist the napkin tight above the quarters. Use the string to tie a knot there.

Disc Golf

What You Do

1 Players create a Disc Golf Course in the house. Use trash cans for the Holes. (That's golf jargon for targets.) The course can go upstairs, downstairs, and all around the house. The Holes will be played in the order you number them, one through nine. The greater the distance between Holes, the longer the game will last.

2 Each player gets a pencil, a scrap of paper, and one Disc (paper dessert plate). Players should initial their Discs. Then players can number from one to nine on their papers to keep track of their points on each round of play.

Number of Players: 2 or more

What You Need: 9 small trash cans or baskets, 1 heavy, sturdy paper or plastic dessert plate per player, 1 pencil per player, 1 scrap of paper per player

Where to Play: throughout the house

The Point: earn a low score

3 Players stand together at an agreed-upon Start Line and take turns trying to get their Discs into the Hole on the first toss. A player who lands a Disc in the Hole has earned a Hole in One and records a perfect score of zero.

4 Any player whose Disc didn't land in the Hole must stand where the Disc landed and toss it again. Take turns making a toss until everyone has gotten a Disc in the Hole. Each player's total number of tosses is her score for the round (other than any perfect zero scores earned from a Hole in One).

5 Play moves to the next Hole. Standing where they were at the end of the first round, or at a new agreed-upon Start Line for this round, players take turns aiming and tossing at the next Hole. Record points the same way.

6 Once all of the Holes have been played, the player with the lowest score wins.

Model

What You Do

1 Players divide into teams with three or more players each. One player on each team puts on an extra shirt, dress, or robe. This player is Model 1. Model 1's clothes should be on correctly, with all buttons buttoned, etc.

2 Model 1 uses one hand to hold the hand of a teammate, who becomes Model 2. The remaining players from each team are the Dressers. They must move the extra clothes from their Model 1 to their Model 2. The models must hold hands the whole time. (This means some of the clothing will be inside out on Model 2.)

Number of Players: 6 or more

What You Need: several old shirts, dresses, or robes

Where to Play: anywhere

The Point: change clothes

3 The first team to move the clothing and re-button all the buttons, etc., wins.

Sam Squeezer

Number of Players: 5 or more
What You Need: scraps of paper, pencil, hat
Where to Play: in a room
The Point: find Sam Squeezer, or squeeze your way to victory

What You Do

1 Tear off a scrap of paper for each player. Mark an X on one. Put the scraps into a hat and have players grab a scrap. Whoever gets the X is Sam Squeezer, but can't tell anyone.

2 The players sit in a circle, memorize who is sitting where, and then grab hold of each other's hands. Players close their eyes for the rest of the game. No peeking. No talking.

3 Beginning from 10 seconds to about a minute later, Sam Squeezer rapidly squeezes one or both of the hands she holds, squeezing one or more times. Players who receive squeezes deduct one squeeze and pass it on.

4 Any player who receives just one squeeze is Out. That player silently lets go and moves away from the circle.

The other players tighten the circle and rejoin hands. Play continues. (The Out player can open his eyes but must remain silent.)

5 A player wins by correctly naming Sam Squeezer. An accused player must truthfully answer "Yes" or "No." Any player who guesses wrong is Out. Play continues—no talking, no peeking.

6 Here's how Sam Squeezer can win: As soon as she sends the squeeze that removes the second-to-the-last player, she must call out "I am Sam Squeezer." If she is accused before she starts speaking, the accusor wins. (In the case of a tie, Sam Squeezer wins.)

I Sit

What You Do

1. The players put the chairs in a wide circle. Players sit down in the chairs. (There's one empty chair.) Then they count out loud together from one to three.

2. After "three," both players on either side of the empty seat try to sit in it first. The slower player returns to his original chair. (If you have trouble deciding who won the seat, assign a Referee to be the judge.)

3. The Winner who got the seat looks around into the eyes of the other players while saying "I sit in the circle with my friend..." At the last moment the Winner looks at just one player and says his name to finish the sentence. ("...Justin!") That named player quickly moves to the Winner's old seat. Meanwhile, the players on either side of the newly emptied seat race to try to sit in it first.

4. The player who fills the empty seat is the Winner, and the game continues until everyone's tired or hungry.

Number of Players: 4 or more

What You Need: chairs for each player, plus 1 extra chair

Where to Play: in a room

The Point: keep track of which seat is empty and fill it—fast!

Scavenger Hunt

Number of Players: 5 or more

What You Need: 1 paper, pencil, and bag per player, a timer or watch

Where to Play: in 1 or more rooms

The Point: find the most stuff

What You Do

1. A player chosen to be Leader makes a list of items to find in the play area. The descriptions should be creative, such as "something square," "something soft," "something clean," "something green," etc.

2. The Leader gathers the players at a Start location and shows the list to the players. The players copy down the list on a piece of paper. If there are a lot of players, they can work in groups. Otherwise, each player gets one list, one pencil, and one bag.

3. When everyone is ready, players agree on a stop time (five minutes for an easy game, longer for a game with lots of objects and a larger area). Then the Hunt begins. Players should move quickly and quietly. When a player finds an item from the list, the player puts it into the bag and marks it off the list.

4. The Leader calls out when time is up, and all players return to Start and show what they found. The Leader decides whether the objects match the descriptions on the list.

5. The player with the most objects from the list wins.

Smuggler

Number of Players: 3 or more
What You Need: 1 backpack, small suitcase, or messenger bag per player, clothes and other items you might take on a trip, one coin per container
Where to Play: in a room
The Point: find the coin

What You Do

1. One player will be the Smuggler. While the other players are looking away, the Smuggler hides one coin in each backpack, and also stuffs each bag full of clothes and other items. The Smuggler zips up or closes the backpacks.

2. The Smuggler then hands one backpack to each player and says, "Go." Players immediately search inside for the hidden coin. None of the contents of the backpack can touch the floor—and the backpack can't touch the floor, either.

3. The first player to find the hidden coin without dropping anything wins.

Limbo......

What You Do

1. Players pick two players to hold the Limbo stick (that's the broom handle or long stick). All of the other players line up behind the stick.

2. The Holders each take one end of the stick and hold it level, about chest-high. The other players walk under the stick by bending backward. Players can't touch the stick, and only their feet can touch the ground.

3. After each round, the Holders lower the stick. The player who can complete the lowest Limbo wins. Remember, nothing but feet may touch the ground!

Number of Players: 4 or more

What You Need: broom handle or long stick

Where to Play: anywhere

The Point: see how low you can go

Stomp

What You Do

1 Each player gets a piece of bubble wrap of similar size. Players count aloud together from one to three. After "three," players stomp as fast as they can to burst all their bubbles.

2 The first player to stomp out all their bubbles wins. Other players can then finish their stomping, just for fun.

Number of Players: 3 or more

What You Need: bubble wrap (it's used to pack fragile items)

Where to Play: in a room

The Point: stomp out all your bubbles

Who Am I?·······

Number of Players: 4 or more
What You Need: name tags, or scraps of paper, pencils, and tape
Where to Play: in a room
The Point: find out who you are

What You Do

1 Players agree on a topic, such as "teachers," "authors," "athletes," "scientists," "book characters," etc. Each player has to be able to think of the name of a person who fits in that topic. (Keep the name a secret for now.)

2 Players find partners. If there's an extra player, there can be one group of three players. Each player writes the name he thought of on a name-tag and sticks it on the back of the partner.

3 When everyone's ready, the game begins. Players start asking questions in order to figure out who they are (whose name is on the name tag). The only answers allowed are "Yes" and "No." Players can move among all players to ask questions. (They don't have to stick with their partner.)

4 Play until all players have guessed their identities. The last player to figure out who he is gets to choose the topic for the next game.

Pick-Up Tug

Number of Players: 3 or more
What You Need: 8 to 10 feet of rope, 1 tissue per player
Where to Play: in a room
The Point: out-pull the opponents

What You Do

1. Players tie the ends of the rope together to make a rope circle. Then they lay the circle in the center of the room.

2. Each player grabs a tissue and sits on the floor outside of the rope circle, sitting an equal distance from the other players.

3. Each player grips the rope with both hands, and holds the rope tight. The rope should be pulled taut, with no slack. (With three players, the rope will be pulled into the shape of a triangle. With four players, the rope forms a square.)

4. One at a time, each player is given just enough slack in the rope to use one free hand to reach as far back as possible and place a tissue there. The tissue must be out of reach when all the players pull the rope tight again.

5 When everyone is ready, begin the game. Players must tug on the rope and try to reach their tissue. The first player to succeed in reaching his tissue wins. There can be second- and third-place winners, too.

6 Players can either pull with both hands or use just one hand. No one can let go of the rope.

Other Ways to Play

Add players: If there are more than 4 players, add 2 to 3 feet of rope and 1 tissue per extra player.

Bogus

Number of Players: 4 or more

What You Need: 20 or more coins or buttons, 1 pen and piece of paper per player

Where to Play: anywhere

The Point: watch your words

What You Do

1. Divide the coins among the players so that players have an equal number of coins. The players should now be silent until the game begins.

2. Players each grab a pen and piece of paper and write down three words. Players should choose words that are commonly used in conversation, or words that they know other players use often, such as "like" or "cool." Players can't choose articles (a, an, the). That's too easy.

3. Players turn their papers over, so no one can see what they wrote, and nod to indicate they are ready to play. When everyone is ready, players begin a conversation and each player tries to steer the other players toward using his word. Every player has to join in the conversation by taking turns speaking. Players should avoid saying the same things repeatedly and keep the conversation going.

4. Anytime a player hears someone saying "his" word, the player reaches a hand to the person who said it. That person must hand over a coin. If more than one player has chosen that word, the player who spoke it must hand out one coin to each player who extends a hand.

5. Players can avoid saying words they think are chosen, but they can't stop taking turns in the conversation. Players are out of the game when they run out of coins. The last player in the game wins.

Clothespins

What You Do

1 Players agree on a time limit for the game, such as three minutes. Use a timer or appoint a Referee who has a watch.

2 Players attach three clothespins to the sleeve or bottom of their shirts. When everyone's ready, the players try to steal the clothespins off other players' shirts. Players can turn or take a single step in any direction to move away to keep someone from stealing their clothespins, but they have to return to their original spot on their next step. Players can't push a hand away or cover or protect clothespins.

Number of Players: 4 or more
What You Need: a timer or watch, lots of clothespins
Where to Play: in a room
The Point: keep your clothespins

3 Players can take only one clothespin at a time from another player. After a player grabs a clothespin, that player must count out loud to three while attaching it to his or her own shirt. During this counting, nobody can steal any of that player's clothespins.

4 When time's up, the player with the most clothespins wins.

Tidal Wave

Number of Players: 5 or more

What You Need: towels of various sizes (hand towels, bath towels, etc.)

Where to Play: in a room

The Point: reach an Island—quick!

What You Do

1 Players scatter the towels around the room, laying them on the floor, unfolded. These towels are the Islands. Every other part of the floor is part of the Sea.

2 One player is the Lookout. The other players are the Castaways. To begin the game, the Castaways stand on the Islands without touching each other. The Lookout can stand anywhere. The Lookout says "The coast is clear." That's the signal for the Castaways to step off the Islands and play in the Sea.

3 The Castaways can pretend to be swimming, diving, or whatever, as long as they are moving around in the Sea. In the meantime, the Lookout removes one Island, any Island, because it has been submerged by a Tidal Wave.

4 At any time after removing an Island, the Lookout yells "Tidal Wave!" That's the signal for the Castaways to rush back onto an Island. No part of their bodies may touch the Sea. No pushing is allowed. Players must share Islands if necessary. Meanwhile, the Lookout counts to three out loud. Castaways who can't find an Island by "three," and any Castaways who are touching, must stay in the Sea for the rest of the game. (The Lookout can be the judge of who stays on an Island and who goes into the Sea.)

5 Play until there's just one Island and one remaining Castaway. The Castaway wins and becomes the new Lookout.

Ultimate Sing-Along

Number of Players: 6 or more
What You Need: flashlight
Where to Play: in a room
The Point: out-sing the competition

What You Do

1 One player is the Emcee. It's best when the Emcee knows all of the players, knows a lot of songs, and likes to act zany. The other players divide into two teams and stand on opposite sides of the room.

2 The Emcee stands in the middle of the room and holds the flashlight.

3 When everyone is in place, the Emcee begins the game by introducing the song to be sung. (The Emcee should pick a popular song that everyone has heard.)

4 The Emcee shines the flashlight on a team. That team starts singing the song. It doesn't matter how it sounds, but the words have to be right. At any time, the Emcee can shine the flashlight on the other team instead. The first team stops singing, and the other team picks up the song.

5 If a team messes up a song or doesn't stop or start on time, they lose a player. The last team still in the game wins.

Who's Got It?

Number of Players: 4 or more
What You Need: a shoe
Where to Play: in a room
The Point: find the Thief

What You Do

1. One player sits in the middle of the room. This is the Detective. The other players sit in a circle around the Detective.

2. The Detective takes off one shoe, closes both eyes, and begins counting to 10. One of the other players picks up the shoe and begins passing it around the circle. Players pass the shoe behind their backs.

3. On the count of 10, the Detective opens both eyes. Everyone must remain seated in place; no wriggling around allowed. As the Detective it's fun to look hard at each player to see who cracks under the scrutiny and questioning. (Players should not say anything in response to the Detective's comments. You have the right to remain silent!)

4. The Detective is allowed to make one accusation and name the Thief. If the Detective correctly guesses who is the Thief, the shoe is returned and the game begins again. If the Detective guesses incorrectly, the Detective closes both eyes again, and play continues.

5. If the Detective guesses wrong three times, the Thief holding the shoe the third time becomes the new Detective.

Shoe Struggle

Number of Players: 4 or more

What You Need: players wearing shoes (it's more fun when they aren't slip-on shoes)

Where to Play: in a room

The Point: get your shoe on first

What You Do

1 Each player takes off one shoe and places it in the middle of the room. Then players form a circle around the pile of shoes and put their arms around the shoulders of the players to the right and left. The players will resemble a team in a huddle.

2 The players move clockwise around the shoes while counting out loud together from one to five. After saying "five," everyone tries to get their own shoe back on, without letting go of the shoulders of the other players.

3 The first player to get her own shoe back on wins.

Other Ways to Play

Double trouble: Players put both shoes in the middle.

Spotlight

What You Do

1. One player is IT. IT picks the music and turns it on. Then IT stands in the middle of the room and holds the flashlight.

2. The other players are Dancers. The Dancers form a loose circle around IT and walk or dance around the circle.

3. Whenever IT wants, IT shines the light on a Dancer. The Dancer has five seconds to dance or silently do something else to make IT laugh.

4. A Dancer wins by making IT laugh. That Dancer becomes the new IT.

Number of Players: 5 or more
What You Need: flashlight, music
Where to Play: in a room
The Point: dance like crazy in the spotlight

Under and Over

Number of Players: 4 or more

What You Need: 1 balloon per pair of players

Where to Play: in a room

The Point: send a balloon down and up and up and down

What You Do

1 Players pair up and stand back to back with their elbows linked. If there's an extra player, let that person be the Referee.

2 One player from each pair holds a balloon between both hands.

3 When the game begins, the pairs pass the balloons first between their legs and then over their heads, back into the hands of the first player.

4 The elbows of the teammates must stay linked. The balloon may not touch the floor.

5 The first team to pass the balloon under and over three times wins.

Winks..............

Number of Players: 4 or more
What You Need: scrap paper, pencil, and hat
Where to Play: anywhere
The Point: beware the Sleeper Wink

What You Do

1 Players sit in a circle. One player tears off one scrap of paper for each player, and draws a small X on just one of the scraps. That player folds each paper scrap, mixes them up, and puts them into the hat.

2 Players draw one paper scrap each, and peek at it. Whoever gets the X is IT and must keep this a secret. All players fold their scraps and put them back into the hat.

3 To start the game, players look at each other cautiously. At any time IT can make eye contact with a player and

wink. This is a Sleeper Wink. A player who is winked at has to close both eyes immediately and slump over. The player is Out of the game and should snore loudly or pretend to be dreaming.

4 If anyone sees IT wink, that player shouts "IT!" and names the player in an accusation, such as "IT! Maria is IT." One other player has to second the accusation. The accused player must tell the truth, and say, "I am IT," or, "I am not IT." If no one seconds the accusation, play continues without any comment from the accused.

5 If the Accusers are wrong, they are both Out of the game and play continues. If the Accusers are correct, they win the game.

Wu-Tan

What You Do

1. One player is the Ninja. The rest of the players are Warriors. The Warriors form a circle around the Ninja, standing at least 3 feet from him.

2. The Ninja does an elaborate bow, and then jumps into action. If the Ninja flings either hand open in the direction of the heads or feet of the Warriors, those Warriors must duck or jump to avoid the Ninja's Flying Daggers. If the Ninja motions as if swinging a Blade at the heads or feet of the Warriors, those Warriors must duck or jump to avoid the Blade. (The Ninja and Warriors can add any sound effects they like.)

3. Any Warrior struck by a combination of Flying Daggers or Blades a total of three times is Out. (If you have trouble agreeing on injuries, assign a Referee to be the judge.) The last remaining Warrior becomes the new Ninja.

Number of Players: 4 or more
What You Need: nothing
Where to Play: in a room
The Point: dodge the Ninja's weapons

Squares

Number of Players: 1 or more
What You Need: a box of toothpicks, timer
Where to Play: on a flat surface
The Point: build a square with the most shapes in it

What You Do

1 Divide the toothpicks among the players. It doesn't matter how many toothpicks you start with. One player sets the timer for one minute and says "Go!"

2 Each player rushes to lay out the toothpicks in square or rectangular patterns. Each player's patterns must work together to create one big square or rectangle. No triangle or other shapes are allowed.

3 When time's up, all players stop. The player with a completed square or rectangle who also has the most shapes within it wins.

Other Ways to Play

Other shapes: Agree to make the shape of a triangle, using only triangles.

Metrics

Need to convert the measurements in this book to metrics? Here's how:

To convert inches to centimeters, multiply by 2.5.
To convert feet to meters, multiply by .3.

Index